Sunrises to Santiago

SUNRISES TO SANTIAGO

SEARCHING FOR PURPOSE ON THE CAMINO DE SANTIAGO

Gabriel Schirm

Sunrises to Santiago

Copyright © 2015 by Gabriel Schirm.

Library of Congress Control Number: 2015908124

ISBN 978-0-9861224-1-5 paperback

Printed in the United States of America

For Amy, my personal guru and best friend

Table of Contents

Author's Note

To write this book, I relied on a personal journal I kept while walking the Camino de Santiago during the summer of 2014. To maintain anonymity, I have changed the names of the characters in this book with the exception of my wife, Amy, who completed this journey with me. In addition to my memory and journal entries, I have included researched facts when I felt they added to the depth and understanding of the story.

Trail Days and Distance

1	St. Jean Pied-de-Port – Roncesvalles	25 km/16 miles
2	Roncesvalles – Zuriain	32 km/20 miles
3	Zuriain – Zariquiegui	23 km/14 miles
4	Zariquiegui – Puente la Reina	13 km/8 miles
5	Puente la Reina – Estella	22 km/14 miles
6	Estella – Los Arcos	21 km/13 miles
7	Los Arcos – Logroño	29 km/18 miles
8	Logroño – Nájera	30 km/19 miles
9	Nájera – Grañon	28 km/18 miles
10	Grañon – Villafranca Montes de Oca	28 km/17 miles
11	Villafranca – Cardeñuela Riopica	24 km/15 miles
12	Cardeñuela Riopica – Burgos	14 km/9 miles
13	Burgos – Hontanas	32 km/20 miles
14	Hontanas – Boadilla del Camino	29 km/18 miles
15	Boadilla del Camino – Carrión de los Condes	27 km/16 miles
16	Carrión – Terradillos de Templarios	27 km/17 miles
17	Terradillos – Calzadilla de los Hermanillos	27 km/17 miles
18	Calzadilla de los Hermanillos – León	43 km/27 miles
19	León	0 km/0 miles
20	León – Villafranca del Bierzo	132 km/82 miles
21	Villafranca del Bierzo – Vega de Valcarce	19 km/12 miles
22	Vega de Valcarce – Hospital de la Condesa	17 km/11 miles
23	Hospital de la Condesa – A Balsa	19 km/12 miles
24	A Balsa – Barbadelo	20 km/12 miles
25	Barbadelo – Portomarín	18 km/11 miles
26	Portomarín – Portos	19 km/12 miles
27	Portos – Boente	26 km/16 miles
28	Boente – Salceda	20 km/12 miles
29	Salceda – Santiago de Compostela	28 km/17 miles

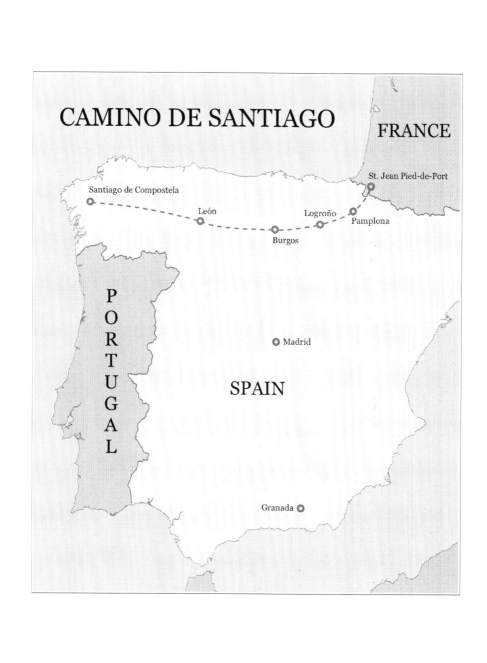

Introduction

Can you use adventure as a form of therapy? Can it be used as a reset button for those who have lost their way? I certainly think so. For me, travel is a way to make space in my life for the answers I seek. Not an escape, but a journey to find personal truth. Perhaps this is why so many have chosen to walk the historic pilgrimage called the Camino de Santiago in Spain. Since the Middle Ages, pilgrims have walked the Camino, asking profound questions about life. The answers, I am certain, have been as varied as the personalities and lives that have experienced this deeply personal journey.

I first learned of the Camino de Santiago while living in the south of Spain with my wife. I am a lover of the great outdoors, and while spending many weekends with new Spanish friends enjoying local *senderos,* or hiking trails, I heard about an incredible personal pilgrimage many of my new friends had completed. Some of them found the experience so meaningful that they had completed the Camino multiple times. The stories of how this journey changed their lives are what inspired me to start planning my own Camino. They told me that I, too, should take on this historic route that crosses their beautiful country. What started as a crazy idea slowly turned into real curiosity. The length of the trail alone seemed like an insurmountable obstacle for my untrained body. I began to seek the advice of my Andalusian friends. I would ask them questions like, "Where should I begin? Can I walk it with my wife? What do you bring? Where do you sleep? Why did you walk? What is the Camino de Santiago, anyway?"

The history and lore of the Camino de Santiago is fascinating. The story begins with St. James, who was one of the 12 apostles of Jesus and one of the first to be martyred.[1] According to the legend, in 40 AD, St. James sailed to Galicia and began his ministry. He preached in Finisterre, the end of the Earth, on the coast of northwestern Spain. This village was sacred and an important location for Druidic rituals. St. James had limited success converting the local pagans to Christianity and returned to Jerusalem where Herod subsequently had him beheaded. The story contends, despite the lack of archeological evidence, that his disciples decided to bring his body back to be buried in Finisterre.

Queen Lupa, who was a powerful pagan monarch at that time, was not happy with this plan. She wanted James's body destroyed and the disciples killed. As the queen's soldiers closed in on the disciples, they were able to escape by crossing the river Tambre just as the bridge collapsed behind them. They escaped to what is now called Santiago, the final resting place of the remains of St. James. As time passed and generations took their turns here on Earth, St. James was all but forgotten.

By the Middle Ages, after the Roman Empire in Spain had lost power, the Muslim community from Morocco started spreading Islam and gaining power in Spain. Life under the Moors was good for a number of years, and the rulers allowed people religious freedom. Christians were generally permitted to practice their faith even under Islamic rule.

The story of St. James only resurfaces again in the year 813 when a bright star led a shepherd named Pelayo to a field near modern-day Santiago where he discovered the hidden tomb of St. James. Hence, a new name for the city was born, Santiago de Compostela. According to the story, Compostela derived from the Latin *Campus Stellae* meaning field of the star.[2] Santiago is a corruption of the Latin *Sanctu Iacobu* (St. James).[3] It is important to note that the legend of Pelayo and his discovery is one of many historical theories.

The local bishop jumped on Pelayo's discovery and declared it to be true. He conveniently used the story of St. James in congruence with the *reconquista* of Spain for Christianity. In subsequent battles, the story goes that the ghost of St. James would appear on the battlefields at just the right moment to help the Christians defeat the Moors. St. James became known as the Moor-slayer or *Santiago Matamoros*. He was particularly good at slicing off soldiers' heads with his sword while riding atop a gallant white steed. Ironic since he himself was beheaded. After all of those years in silence, he quickly became the patron saint of Spain, a title that he still enjoys today.

So when did people start walking to Santiago de Compostela to pay their respects? The first historical record of a pilgrimage happened in 950 when Bishop Gotescalco made the journey. This route became increasingly popular among pilgrims in the twelfth and fourteenth centuries. When the Holy Land was no longer accessible to Christians, the Camino de Santiago became *the* pilgrimage for Christians. Thousands upon thousands of people decided to make the pilgrimage during the Middle Ages. Many simply walked out their front doors, beginning in Paris, Barcelona, Geneva, Granada, Sevilla and of course St. Jean Pied-de-Port, and made their way to the incredible cathedral in Santiago de Compostela where the relics of St. James rested, and still remain to this day.[4]

Today, people walk this route for a number of reasons, some religious and others for personal growth. An adventure trek across the north of Spain sounded exactly like what I needed. An incurable wanderlust had led me to the south of Spain after I had (once again) escaped the monotony of an unfulfilling job back in the United States. The recent celebration of my 30th birthday only amplified my angst. My least favorite party question to be asked was, "So, what do you do?"

I watched my friends and spouse becoming accomplished professionals. I wondered why I couldn't seem to get it together. I started to wonder if I would ever work at a job I truly enjoyed and, by extension, find my life's passion. I had already spent my 20s traveling and trying on hats that never really fit. It was time for a change.

I am not a deeply religious person but if pressed would define myself as spiritual. I had high hopes that walking the Camino de Santiago and communing with nature would also help answer the questions I needed answered. I had uncertainty not only about my career but also deeper questions that I had always pushed to the back of my mind. *What is the meaning of life? Why am I here? What is my purpose here on Earth?* A tall order, I know, but I decided that the answers to my questions were waiting for me somewhere in the north of Spain.

This book chronicles a journey of personal growth on the Camino de Santiago and an incredible adventure. From the physical high of crossing the magnificent Pyrenees Mountains to the mind numbing rhythm of walking through the summer heat of the *Meseta*. From challenges like bed bugs and tendinitis to emotional scars that would lead to elusive answers. The lessons were all around. Who knew thousands of vivid colors greet each day before a Spanish sunrise? Or that with a simple pencil, a kind man in Galicia could teach me lessons about my own journey through life?

Did I find the answers to all of my questions? Absolutely, but not in the way I had planned. The answers to my questions came from the amazing experiences and conversations I had with fellow pilgrims from all over the world. My body suffered greatly. My mind was tested and my spirit broken at times. This experience changed who I am, and I decided to write it all down.

PART ONE

THE WALKING STICK

I cried every day for the first
week because the pain was incredible.

Kate, Pilgrim from Seattle
Trail Day 4

It's about the Way,
not about the destination.

Anonymous, Written on a Stone Near Estella
Trail Day 5

Arrival

It is a homecoming of sorts, but I couldn't feel farther away from home. *Pamplona*. I spot the large black and white airport sign shining in the afternoon sun. It looks as if it has been polished just for our arrival. After a 20-hour day of travel, my brain is foggy, but we manage to grab a cab. I am overjoyed to be back in Spain and quickly practice my rusty Spanish with our taxi driver. "¡Hola, buenas!" I yell as we throw our packs in the back of the cab.

As we begin to make our way to the hotel, I enthusiastically tell the driver, "¡Mañana vamos a empezar el Camino de Santiago!" *Tomorrow we are going to begin the Camino de Santiago!* He looks at me with a big grin and says, "I know." I guess our clothes and backpacks gave us away.

I gaze out of the window, and my mind flashes back to two years earlier as my wife Amy and I sat in our small apartment in Granada, Spain. The memory still fresh and vivid in my mind. Tears streamed down her face as she applied an ice pack to her fractured fibula, just above the left ankle. Bitter disappointment filled the room. Our half packed backpacks lay on the floor, and a guidebook for the Camino de Santiago seemed to mock us from its place on the table. We were supposed to leave that day to begin the Camino, which would have been the culmination and end to our two year adventure of living in Spain. A night of dancing after our goodbye party ended all of those grand plans when Amy quite literally busted a move on the dance floor. I told her not to worry, not quite believing myself. We will get to go someday. Everything happens for a reason.

"We are here," the cabdriver says, interrupting my daydream.

I turn back to the cabdriver and offer a smile. He hands us our backpacks and with true sincerity shakes my hand, looks me directly in the eyes, and says, "Buen Camino peregrinos," which basically means *happy trails* or *have a good walk*. *Peregrino* is Spanish for *pilgrim*.

After our overnight stay in Pamplona, we catch the bus to our chosen starting point for this journey: St. Jean Pied-de-Port in France. By midafternoon, after a nausea-inducing bus ride over winding mountain roads, Amy and I find ourselves at the beginning of a long planned adventure three years in the making. The Camino Frances. Of the many routes to Santiago de Compostela, the Camino Frances is by far the most famous and subsequently the most popular. We hop off the bus with a handful of Camino strangers and make our way to the pilgrim's office to obtain our "pilgrim passports."

These official documents are required if you want to stay in the network of *albergues* (pronounced al-BEAR-gays) or pilgrim hostels that are found along the Camino. These simple budget accommodations are reserved for pilgrims only and will provide us with a bed, a shower, a roof, and basic necessities. The special passports could have also been ordered by mail, but I am trying to approach this adventure without much planning. The colorful stamps that you collect from the pilgrim hostels each day will be the evidence you present upon arrival in Santiago de Compostela to prove you have actually completed your journey and thus receive your *Compostela* (certificate of completion).

The pilgrim's office is bustling with new arrivals eager to begin their journey. There is a row of tables set up inside, each staffed by a volunteer. I hear four or five different languages being spoken at the same time, and the electric feeling of excitement is palpable. Each volunteer shouts out a language when they are finished helping a pilgrim and it is the next person's turn: "Frances! Español! English!" We make our way to the English table and take a seat. Each passport costs 2 euro and is handed to us encased in a small plastic baggie.

"For the rain," our helpful volunteer explains. "But you are lucky because the weather forecast is calling for sun tomorrow. Crossing the Pyrenees is best during sunny days. You will love the views. Do you have somewhere to stay tonight?" she asks. I hadn't even thought about it, and my look gives me away. She quickly calls up an albergue in town and books us two beds. Easy enough.

We slowly make our way to the albergue through this small French town. The old stone buildings form walls on either side of the cobble-stone streets, and a wide river runs through the center of town. We take our time crossing over an old stone bridge that connects both sides of the river. Brightly colored flowers grow in planter boxes hanging from windowsills, and vines crawl up some of the walls, easily finding anchors in the somehow perfect cracks. Beyond the city center, the town is surrounded by lush green hills and mountains. We both look around through the rose-colored eyes of travelers, and big grins spread across our faces. A woman wearing an apron steps out of her quaint little bakery and waves, "Bonjour."

We finally find our albergue and are greeted by a cheery French woman with rosy cheeks and a charming accent. She declares, "I am the famous Amandine. Welcome! Breakfast will be ready at six o'clock tomorrow morning. Now, I will show you your beds."

Amandine shows us to our room, which contains about 20 beds and leaves us to choose our own. I place my hat on my chosen bed next to a large window as a sign it has been claimed. We grab our large Camino backpacks and decide to go find some food before settling in for the night. The famous Amandine stops us as we walk past the front door. "What are you doing with your bags?" she asks in her thick French accent, clearly confused.

I didn't see anywhere to lock them and reply, "So no one takes them."

She laughs and orders us to march back upstairs and leave the bags. "No one will steal your packs peregrinos. You have a long way to walk, you shouldn't be taking your backpacks with you to dinner. They don't need the calories as much as you do!"

We grab a baguette and a *gâteau* for dessert from a small shop as the sun starts to go down. Taking a seat outside near the small bridge in the city center, I am finally relaxed enough to take in the scene. The *gâteau*, a tart from the Basque region of France, is filled with pastry cream and brandied cherries. A light buttery crust envelopes a perfectly sweet, tart, and creamy center. It is absolutely delicious. The golden rays of the setting sun cast long shadows over the cobble-stone streets, and as we eat, we listen to the river below. A beautiful midsummer European scene.

"Why is French bread so good? Seriously, what do they put in this stuff?" Amy asks with her mouth full of baguette.

A man walks by with wife and small daughter in tow and offers a friendly, "Bon appétit."

"Gracias," I reply as Amy slaps me on the shoulder.

"We are in France, not Spain, you idiot! Wrong language," she jokes.

I am giddy with excitement, fear, and butterflies as Amy and I start to strategize our plan of attack for tomorrow. We decide getting a good night's sleep is definitely the best way to begin this adventure and head back to the albergue early.

The room had filled to capacity with pilgrims while we were gone. I have never experienced such a somber and quiet mood in a hostel before. After the polite "holas" and "hi how are yous" everyone is completely silent as we all become lost in our heads contemplating the long road ahead. A thousand thoughts swirl around the room like a silent swarm of bees. Some feverishly write in journals and others simply stare at the ceiling while lying on their beds. Many are lost in prayer, their lips moving silently with their thoughts.

We have given ourselves 30 days, a slightly quicker pace than most, to walk from St. Jean Pied-de-Port to Santiago de Compostela. This journey will take us approximately 490 miles through the northern part of Spain. My head fires off questions as I lie down, trying to get some sleep. *What will it be like? Will I find the answers to my questions? Who will I meet? Will Amy and I fight? Will I be physically able to make it?*

Tomorrow we cross the Pyrenees Mountains and the French-Spanish border. As the sun sets and the lights go out, I cannot sleep. I feel a large pit form in my stomach as I wrestle with nerves. Rest never comes as I am lost in my thoughts. Tomorrow we begin.

Euphoria

Before the sun is up, our room is bustling with life. I glance out the window, and through the morning fog I spot two pilgrims silently gliding past below. A shock of electricity hits me. This is actually happening! No one speaks as we pack our backpacks and head downstairs to start the day with what is arguably the worst breakfast ever. Black burnt toast and coffee with the flavor of funk. We drink our coffee from a cereal bowl as our cheery French *hospitalera*, the famous Amandine, tells us the custom of this region. "We use bowls because it is easier to dip your croissant in your coffee," she explains.

We gulp down the funk, strap on our 7-kilo packs (15.4 pounds) and after three years of planning we are finally walking! I am filled with adrenaline and our beginning pace, despite everyone warning us to take it easy, is quick. We start a beautiful climb through forests, fields, and increasingly spectacular views of the lush green Pyrenees Mountains.

We walk relatively alone during the morning hours, and I immediately notice the peaceful feeling of just walking. The hikers are all still mostly quiet and contemplative as they walk. Amy shares her mantra for the day, which I adopt, "I am light and I am strong.

I have all of the answers I need inside of me." I am apparently married to Buddha or at the very least a much wiser soul than I. My focus shifts back to this thought off and on for the next few hours.

I already find myself deep in thought, hoping to be hit on the head with a bright flashing light offering me the clarity I am seeking on this trip. What is my next move? I spent my 20s as a radio disc jockey, Travel Channel host, videographer, webmaster, and recruiter for a study abroad program. Those sound like great gigs—and they were—but nothing panned out.

I loved hosting a radio show, and landing the night show at a big top 40 station in town was the best job any junior in college could ask for. I remember the first time someone asked me for my autograph. It was thrilling and an immediate drug-like injection straight to my ego. I wanted more. I graduated from Colorado State University and landed a job as a travel journalist on the Travel Channel. I got to travel the world, be on TV, and get paid for it. It was exciting: photo shoots in Los Angeles, press conferences in Hong Kong, and when I got back home, even more people stopped me for photos and autographs. Life was good. But alas, the show was temporary, and I had to figure out what I wanted to do next. I tried radio again, but it felt different and somehow stale. I wasn't fulfilled, so I quit and felt crazy for doing so.

I relocated to Denver to move in with Amy as things were getting the way they do when you fall in love. I got a job for CBS updating their websites with content, but after four long months, I told Amy that it was a job that "crushed my soul." So again, I quit.

The insanity escalated. I begged for my previous radio job back. I remember being so lost in a constant state of anxiety not knowing which direction to turn. I met with my old boss and tried to explain why after having quit my hosting gig on his radio station's morning show only four months ago it was a good idea to take me back. I explained how CBS crushed my soul, how things would be different, how I had found my passion for radio again and why I deserved a second chance. He told me he would have to convince a lot of people that it was a good idea to take me back. After a week, I was offered that second chance, and in an epic move of career suicide, I turned down the job. I told him I had changed my mind, again.

I buried myself in self-help books. *What Color Is Your Parachute?* I had no idea. I took career tests, made endless lists of possible jobs including ridiculous options like helicopter pilot and career coach. Amy helped me realize that being a career coach was probably not a great idea for someone in my situation. She suggested maybe I go see a career coach for some advice instead. More than once I wondered if I should ask for a third chance with my old boss. Thankfully, I thought better of that idea.

Leveraging my video skills and radio background, I eventually landed a job creating video content for a cluster of Denver radio stations, and it was fun. I got to interview big name bands, host a weekend show, and produce entertaining video content for the station's listeners. But instead of the rush I used to get from being in this exciting world, I felt like a fish out of water. For me it lacked purpose, and the agony of feeling like you are not on your true path is hard to handle. I became frustrated with the advice that I should follow my passion. "Don't worry, just go for it," my well meaning friends would say. But I didn't know what *it* was. If I did, I would have been going for *it*!

As we trek up a steep trail, questions about life bounce around in my head: *Do I start a business like I have always wanted? What about the risk? What business would I even start?* The true question underneath them all continues to surface: *What is my purpose in this life?* I am now 32 and desperately in need of direction. We stop for a break to take it all in, and I try to focus on keeping my head clear. I grab the small journal from my pack and decide to write. For me this is a calming exercise. Writing is a sort of meditation.

Amy and I sit for a while, listening to the birds singing, the rustle of the trees swaying in the wind, and the soft call of the mountain sheep that are hidden in the clover-covered hills. Watching the clouds roll around themselves below us, stress melts away. Even the blades of grass and honey-bees buzzing from flower to flower seem to add to the perfect symphony of sound.

"What if we want to do this again?" Amy breaks the silence.

"Let's make it through one day before we start to plan our next trip," I say and smile in return. And then doze off into an unplanned nap. I wake up, surprised to see Amy in downward dog.

"What are you doing?" I ask.

"What does it look like?" she replies. "Yoga. Stretching feels so good!"

I shake my head and sit up to take a look around. There are a handful of pilgrims pointing and giggling as they pass. Amy was going to bring her yoga mat with her, a point of contention in our planning process. I ultimately won, convincing her that the weight would be worse for her joints than the benefit of actually doing yoga. She has apparently decided to use the soft grass as her yoga mat.

"Well get it in now. I don't think we will be able to move with so much ease in a few days," I say. She has made her way to tree pose.

"Nonsense. This is precisely why I will be able to move with ease in a few days, you'll see," she argues while twisting into a pretzel.

This stage has an elevation climb of 1,390 meters (4,560 feet), and we make it to our high point of 1,450 meters (4,757 feet) after six hours of trekking, snapping pics, and setting our quick pace. Near the summit, I spot a fellow pilgrim with a bright white beard and notice something peculiar. He is walking barefoot. I notice the look of happiness on his face. His pace is similar to ours so we walk "with" him for about an hour.

He takes time to dip his feet in a mountain stream, feel the grass between his toes, and every once in a while pauses to take a deep breath of fresh mountain air. He looks euphoric and completely at peace surveying the incredible mountain scenery. The weather could not be better and the panoramic views of the mountains all around us are breathtaking. He sits near us as we take in a particularly spectacular view and decide to have a snack. "Beeeuuteefull yaw!" he yells to us in broken English. I nod back with a giant smile in agreement.

Here is a man who has a simple pack and no shoes, while I spent months debating between hiking shoes or trail running shoes. I agonized over what backpack would be most comfortable and purchased specialized socks that allow your feet to breathe yet stay insulated. I laugh at myself and mentally thank him for teaching me to not take things so seriously.

After our break, I yell, "Buen Camino" to our nameless friend and continue on. I can already feel the effects of walking with a pack, so we decide to take it slow on the steep descent into Roncesvalles, which proves to be more challenging than the ascent. Most injuries happen here as still excited pilgrims descend too quickly with their heavy packs. Small tears in your tendons begin and develop into more serious problems with every step you take.

We arrive in Roncesvalles after roughly 11 hours of walking and my feet are absolutely on fire. I collapse at the first bar and grab two beers as we survey the damage. One blister on Amy's left foot and both of my feet are aching. Despite the pain, I am loving this adventure. We sit outside enjoying two *pintxos,* or small snacks, and chatting with fellow pilgrims who all have the same look on their faces as we do: tired bliss.

I notice my left knee is really hurting. I have never experienced this type of pain in my left knee, and the feeling of regret slowly creeps into my mind. I wish we would have taken today more slowly. Amy shares with me her lesson of the day, "I am not invincible, even though I try to be. Humility is key."

"My knee really hurts," I say, trying to dismiss my worry.

"I am sure it will be better tomorrow," Amy replies.

As a Colorado native who grew up hiking in the Rocky Mountains I assumed that this trek would be completely possible with no training at all. Maybe I was wrong. Maybe I should have trained. This might be harder than we both thought.

"Ouch!" Amy painfully winces as she takes off her shoes and socks, tending to her blister.

"Need the blister kit?" I ask.

"I guess," she replies in frustration. "Seriously! I can't believe I have to use the kit already." She quickly gets to work on her new little friend.

The albergue for the night is an enormous stone building with 183 beds divided into four rooms. We pay our 10 euro apiece and hand over our pilgrim passports to receive our first stamp. We start to head upstairs to find our beds when one of the workers yells at us.

"Shoes off!" he scolds us.

"Oh. Sorry I didn't know," I reply. "Where do we put them?"

We are shown a large room full of hundreds of pairs of shoes. "Just don't forget where you put them!" the man jokes.

Upstairs the bunks are separated into cubicles of four and as we set down our packs, we meet our cube mates. John from New Orleans and a kind older German man who does not speak any English or Spanish, so we communicate through gestures and smiles. He speaks to us a lot in German over the course of the evening even though we have no idea what he is saying. It always amazes me that you really can have a conversation without having a clue what exactly the other person is saying.

"We have a problem," Amy says returning from the greeting area downstairs. "Remember how our shampoo got tossed by TSA at the airport? Well, the people downstairs say that the closest place to buy shampoo is about a day's walk away. Since we planned to use the shampoo for soap as well, we don't have anything to clean off today's yuck."

"There is hand soap in the bathrooms. I guess we can use that," I joke. "We are roughing it now!"

After a hand soap shower, we head out to dine on our first *menú del peregrino,* or pilgrim menu, at one of the two restaurants in town. For 9 euro, we eat a simple but delicious meal. A pilgrim menu is basically a special meal for pilgrims that most restaurants offer along the Way. It is similar to the normal *menú del dia,* or menu of the day, you find all over Spain but usually is a little cheaper. It typically consists of a first course, second course, bread and dessert, and usually includes a bottle of wine. The cost is typically only 7 to 10 euro so the price for the much needed high calorie meals is quite good.

The dinner is communal style and starts with simple pasta and chorizo, followed by fresh river trout, dessert, bread and a bottle of red wine. We sit with a group from Italy and France who have all done the Camino de Santiago before and assured us, "This will change your life!" I tell them our plan of walking further than the recommended stage tomorrow, and they beg us to reconsider.

"I am serious, Gabe," a concerned Italian man tells me as everyone nods in agreement. "Don't walk too far tomorrow. Why are you walking the Camino anyway?"

"It's stupid I guess," I reply, feeling a bit sheepish sharing something so personal with people I have known for less than an hour. "I need focus. I need to know what my purpose is. I need to know what career I should pursue. I need to know why I am here. Here on Earth, that is."

"This is not stupid," the Italian man replies with a slight smile. "We are all here for different reasons. Be open to the lessons you will discover on your way to Santiago. Don't force the answers, and don't forget this is not a race so take it slow." I nod in agreement.

Church bells ring loudly from somewhere outside and another woman from Italy asks, "Time for Mass. Would you like to come?"

"No thanks, not today," I politely decline.

We say our goodbyes as the entire table heads outside, leaving Amy and me alone. The concern on their faces has planted a seed of doubt and fear in my mind. I have only pretended to consider their requests to walk less tomorrow. I would soon learn that we should have listened to their advice.

The Barista

It has been a while since I have slept on the top bunk of a bunk bed, and I am beginning to see that sleep deprivation may lead to possible hallucinations on this trek. My un-needed alarm goes off at 5:00 a.m., and I look around to see many pilgrims already heading out the door. Amy and I stuff our sleeping bags quietly into our packs and slip outside before dawn. We are greeted by a dark, damp sky and a wet path as it has rained all night. I spot a sign on the way out of town, *Santiago de Compostela - 765 km.* I glance at Amy and point to the sign. She is not amused. We both clearly need coffee. We sleep walk for hours through a thick forest as the day slowly turns from dark to light. Finally we see a bar and grab our first *café con leche* of the day, coffee with steamed milk.

The caffeine starts to wake me and I start to become aware of my body. My left knee is still killing me. I try to squash a bit of panic as I think about how far we still have left to go. This is only day two of 30!

After breakfast, we stumble onward and keep seeing a group of four guys we briefly met the first day in St. Jean. They were staying at our first albergue, and we recognize each other. They are from Hungary and decided a few weeks ago to walk the Camino de Santiago. We say "Buen Camino" and end up talking to them as we walk for a few hours. I immediately connect with one in particular as I am quickly realizing that the people you meet on the Way are a huge part of this international experience. So many people from so many walks of life walk the Camino for a myriad of reasons.

His friends jokingly call him The Barista, and I find out why as we end up talking about coffee for about an hour. He is passionate about the topic and is also a youth pastor in a church back home. He just had his first child (we are the same age) and is clearly a proud new father.

"So, why are you here walking the Camino de Santiago?" I ask as we walk.

"I have a big decision in life," he explains slowly in English, his second language. "I am a youth pastor in Hungary. I also love coffee. My dream is to have a coffee shop with books and to speak with people from all over the world as they drink my delicious brews."

"That sounds amazing," I reply as we continue on a wide dirt trail through a thick oak forest. Amy is a ways back chatting with the rest of the group.

"Yes, but I am a pastor and I don't know if I can do both," he explains.

"So you are looking for your answer out here in the woods?" I ask.

"I want God to tell me what to do," he replies with a big smile.

"Maybe you can do both?" I suggest. "Be a pastor and have a coffee shop."

"Maybe. Maybe. I don't know," he replies as we enter a clearing and take in a big blue sky. There is not a cloud in sight. The June summer sun beats down on us all, and both The Barista and I take a second to wipe the sweat from underneath our large straw hats. I can tell that he is really struggling with this decision, somehow stuck between what he wants to do and what he is supposed to do.

"What do you do?" he asks.

"Nothing important," I reply. "I am trying to figure things out." We pause for a sip of water. The Barista kneels down and stirs the dirt on the trail with a stick as if digging for an answer.

"Nothing important huh. You know the human ego is a funny thing," he says. "Everyone has a purpose. If you ask me, Americans are too focused on becoming better than their friends. It is human nature of course. In Hungary we do the same. But be careful with thinking like this."

"Why do you want a coffee shop?" I ask.

"Because I know I will enjoy it, and I am in love with coffee. The smell of the dark brown beans roasting, brewing and dripping into a perfect cup. The white steam rising from a mug on a cold morning. Holding the hot cup in your hands, letting it warm up your soul. It is not easy to make a good cup of coffee you know. It is an art form. You Americans have bad coffee!"

"Hey now!" I protest.

"I especially love good, um, what is the word in English? Fim. No. Fime. Foam! Milk foam! Good milk foam on the coffee, steamed to perfection. I love that. I want this not because it will make me a success in the eyes of others you see, but because it brings me joy. To remain a pastor also gives me a sense of helping and joy. But you must be careful. I am no better than those who ask me for spiritual advice," he explains. "What do your parents do for work?"

"My mom cleans houses, and my dad was a carpenter. He also had a restaurant at one time. He named it after me," I reply. "But he has been struggling lately. He was sober for 20 years and well, not anymore. He has been homeless for the last few years. He lives in his truck." I search The Barista's face and am surprised by his response.

"Your dad is a, what is the word in English? A renegade. Yes, a renegade, no?" he replies with a smile. "You clearly love them both. I can see pain, though, in your eyes."

"Yeah I guess. It is an odd thing to watch your parents struggle. I just want them to be happy, you know," I reply. "They are both good people. They both sort of shun society. Hippies, I guess, but I appreciate that a lot now. It is funny. Growing up my dad looked like ZZ Top. He had a huge beard, and sometimes it would embarrass me. I guess all kids are embarrassed by their parents growing up. For me, it was just because other dads were clean-shaven and more by the book. Now that I am older, I hate cookie cutter. I love people who are different and have interesting stories to tell. People who have failed, overcome or gone through challenging experiences."

"It sounds like they taught you a great lesson about life," he replies. "Different is good. It is so funny how people always want to be superior though you know. I read a book about this recently. It simply teaches you a simple lesson about wanting to be better than others. You know, employees and their bosses, politicians and average citizens, bus drivers and passengers, or even the person bagging your groceries. People who have homes and people who don't," he jokes.

"So what was the lesson of the book?" I ask.

The Barista pauses in some shade for effect and says, "Make sure you always have something to learn from people or else they become your enemy. Everyone has something to teach you. Once you master that line of thinking you will be both happier, and you will also not answer my question in the way you did before."

"What do you mean?" I reply confused.

"I asked what do you do, and you said nothing important," he explains. "You have something to teach people. I am learning from you right now. Don't sell yourself so short. Have you ever met anyone important?" I look at him and nod in acknowledgment as we wind our way through the woods.

"I have. I used to interview a lot of famous people. I guess they are important," the words sound wrong as I say them.

"What did you think of the important people?" He asks. I think about this for a few minutes before replying.

"I didn't like most of them to be honest. They also thought they were important. It doesn't make someone fun to be around when they believe they are more important than you," I say. The Barista smiles.

"You see! You know the answers to your own questions. You just don't know it yet," he pats me on the shoulder.

The Barista is a foodie and a philosopher. This Hungarian is my kind of guy. I am trying to soak up all of my conversations on this trip, and I love what he has shared about his approach to life.

Because of my slower pace and knee pain that seems to be getting worse, we finally separate and wish them a buen Camino. Who knows if we will see them again. We just spent about an hour talking and walking. The Barista looks back with a concerned look on his face.

"Will we see you again?" he yells back. "I want to share a good cup of coffee!"

"I hope so!" I yell back. "We will see you again on the trail!" We continue on, limping past the recommended stopping point in Larrasoaña.

As I put one foot in front of the other, I can't help but think about the millions of people over thousands of years who have walked this very trail. The ghosts of pilgrims past seem to walk with you and encourage you on. Centuries of hopes, dreams, and questions have made this trek. If only these trees could talk.

After another hour or so, I literally cannot walk any more. My left knee is throbbing, and we stop on the edge of a waterfall to soak our feet. The cool water feels like morphine rolling over my aching bones.

As we rest, a man who is the spitting image of Santa Claus rounds the corner. A giant of a man who must be at least 6 feet, 5 inches tall with a big white beard and a Robin Hood hat complete with a feather sticking out the top. He says hello with a thick British accent.

A very peaceful soul, he is from Austria, and as we talk, his voice soothes me just like the cool water running over my feet. He has already been walking for four weeks and started somewhere in the middle of France. "Too many people on this part of the Camino," he says with a frown. Just like that, he says buen Camino and is gone.

Gingerly putting my shoes back on and hobbling back to the trail, we start again. I feel like a 90-year-old man struggling to move forward. A metal walker sounds like an enticing idea. After only five minutes, a pleasant surprise awaits us around the corner. A brand new albergue that is not in the guidebook! We check in and after a full day—10 hours or so—of walking we pay for two beds and slump into chairs. John from New Orleans, our cube mate from last night's albergue, surprises me with a slap on the back! "How ya doin?"

"Hey!" I say, surprised to see him again staying at this random albergue. "My knee is killing me, to be honest."

He examines the swelling of my left knee with a grimace on his face. "That doesn't look too good. It's settled then." Not allowing me to argue, he kindly trades us our bunk beds in the communal room for his private room he had booked for himself. A small, wonderful act of kindness.

After showers and laundry, which is done in a sink, we go downstairs to enjoy a well deserved communal style dinner with new friends. Working around the large rectangle table, we meet the dinner guests, which include a father and son from Spain. They are walking a section of the Camino together to bond before the son heads off to university. Seated next to them is a man from France who introduces himself in English, "I am Adrien. Nice to meet you." Adrien is middle-aged, has salt and pepper hair, is tall, and is in very good shape.

John joins us and finally we meet the albergue owner and his wife, who have carefully prepared our Spanish feast. Tonight's conversation is in Spanish and broken English. Adrien does not speak either well, so we speak slowly. The conversation is rich as we stuff our faces full of chicken simmered in tomatoes and olives. There are enough bottles of wine on the table to satisfy a small army, and I can start to feel the physical pain of the day melt away with each sip. It feels good. "So, Adrien, why are you here?" I ask.

"Ummm I, a girl. Mmm a," he struggles to find the words in English.

"Girl problems!" John proclaims, laughing as he refills everyone's glasses to the brim with wine. "Amen, bother!" His glass clings against Adrien's as a way to say, Welcome to the club. Adrien continues with a grin on his face.

"My wife, yes?" he asks making sure he has found the right word.

"Wife, yes. You are married?" Amy encourages him to continue. He has the full attention of the table.

"My wife. I am here to. How do you say?" He pauses to retrieve the word from somewhere in his brain. "I am here to get away from her."

Silence. "To get *away* from her?" I ask emphasizing the word *away*.

"Yes, away? Not with her," he repeats. "She is. Umm. What is the word? Yes. Evil."

Suddenly the room bursts into riotous laughter. I have not laughed this hard in quite some time. Poor Adrien looks very confused as he has just shared something personal and can't quite understand why we are all laughing so hard. This of course makes me laugh harder.

"Well, here's to that evil woman!" John stands up and toasts to the room. I stand up to join him in the toast and when I stand up an unexpected sharp line of electric pain shoots from my knee, through my hip and directly to my vocal cords. I let out an uncontrolled, raw groan that is far too loud to hide. "Eeeeehhhhhhhhh-haaww!" I am stunned by the sound that has just come out of my own mouth. Embarrassed, I look around the room. The laughter erupts again, even louder than before.

"¡Es la hora de acostarte hombre viejo!" The owner of the albergue says as he grins. *It is time for bed, old man.*

In the morning, my abs hurt from laughter. Evidence that we had an amazing night with new friends. Amy is seated trailside in the shade of a large tree. "Still damp," she says as she repositions her clothes, which we washed last night. They are now secured with wooden clothespins to the outside of her pack. A walking dryer. "How ya feelin, old man?" she asks.

"Ha ha very funny. I can feel my heartbeat in my knee. I am getting worried," I say. The pain in my knee is almost unbearable today. "I looked on Google last night, and I have come to the conclusion that I am completely screwed. The internet said that people seriously injure themselves on the Camino."

"We get to choose our attitude. Worrying is praying for what you don't want," she says as I fuss over my injuries.

"Ok, ok," I reply. "You have a point." I am angry this morning and feeling sorry for myself.

Amy's body is in pain too, and she explains that the outside tendon of her right knee just feels wrong. The euphoria of day one is gone as the expectations start to fade into reality.

Hours pass as we make our way west, and by noon we make it to Pamplona. Due to its ease of access, many pilgrims choose Pamplona as their starting point for the Camino de Santiago, instead of St. Jean. Made famous by Ernest Hemingway's 1926 novel *The Sun Also Rises*, today this city enjoys worldwide fame for the running of the bulls during the San Fermín festival, held annually from July 6th to the 14th. Pamplona also shares deep ties to the Camino de Santiago and has served as a stopping point for pilgrims over the centuries.[1] Many people we have met along the Way plan to stay in Pamplona for a rest day to enjoy the sites. We don't have the luxury of time, unfortunately, so we'll be enjoying Pamplona briefly as we pass through.

We admire the gates of the city when my knee again begins to scream. Every time I put weight on my left knee, a fire ignites directly under my kneecap. "I cannot walk anymore!" I tell Amy. "Let's take a break."

Full of fear, for the first time I begin to seriously think to myself, *I might not be able to finish this.* I start to feel sorry for myself. This is only day three! I try to describe the symptoms to Amy. I see fear in her eyes, too, as she looks at my knee, which is beginning to swell. She is normally the calm one, and the look on her face scares me even more. Could three years of planning end this quickly?

Just at this low point of the day, sitting on a sad bench at the gates of Pamplona, we see our Hungarian crew round the corner. I am glad to see them.

"I told you I would see you again," I joke to my foodie friend The Barista.

"You will be glad you did," he answers as he starts to pull out some seriously amazing stuff from his pack. "Eat," he says. I am starting to think I need to visit Hungary.

He pulls out a little jar and sprinkles the contents into my out-stretched palm.

"Bee pollen," he explains. "It is good for the immune system."

He follows this with some homemade sausage and peach seeds. I didn't even know you could eat peach seeds. I devour the small brown nuts, which are a bit smaller than an almond and delicious! The sausage is good, too, and I ask with my mouth full, "What kind of meat is this? It is so good!"

One of The Barista's friends replies with a straight face, "Horse meat." My chewing slows, and I shoot Amy a look of barely con-cealed panic. They all bust into laughter as I realize the joke is on me.

"So," The Barista says. "Your knee doesn't look too good."

The Barista's pack is full of supplies, and he and his friends quickly get to work. He pulls out an extra knee brace, ibuprofen cream, and a magnesium drink tablet. His friend starts to crack me up as he tells Amy, "Don't worry, we are Hungarian doctors," which we already know they clearly are not. It is amazing how the Camino provides exactly what you need right when you need it. This was the first of many serendipitous moments that I won't soon forget.

"Things are about to get weird," one says to the group and grabs my leg. He elevates it and rubs the pain cream into my knee.

"Did you train for the Camino de Santiago?" I ask with a bit of regret since I did not.

They continue to keep me laughing as one replies, "Yes of course, I started taking the stairs at work!"

After 10 minutes, they say goodbye and leave me reeling. The kindness of new friends. My spirits are lifted, and we begin to gin-gerly hobble on again. One step at a time. The knee brace and pain cream combination helps tremendously as we continue through

Pamplona. The lesson of the day is clear. It is OK to let people help you. The Camino will provide.

Pamplona is a beautiful bustling city of 200,000 people.[2] We take our time winding through the narrow streets, weaving through locals busily going about their day, and eventually we make our way out of town. As the afternoon sun bears down, sweat starts to drip down my sunglasses. It is incredibly hot. We enter brown fields of wheat with no shade in sight and trudge on and on over the dry dirt path.

As we walk, I immediately notice the bugs. Tiny black shiny squiggling bugs keep sticking to the sweat on our arms as we walk. No matter how much we try to brush them off they just kept coming, hour after hour as we forge ahead. It is safe to say that I am pissed off again. Hot, tired, and covered in disgusting gnats from the fields, which seem to be getting worse as we go. I give up trying to get them off and just let them multiply.

"Well, this is a romantic walk today, isn't it?" I yell to Amy who is far ahead on the trail.

We pass by some ancient ruins and make our way up the final ascent of the day to our new destination. We had planned to walk much further but it is clear I cannot. We spot our Hungarian friends for the second time today resting next to a water fountain up ahead. One makes his way back from the village to offer to carry my pack. I am again caught off guard by this kindness and feel like a weakling. Backtracking on the Camino is a big deal. We check into our albergue for the night, and I am looking forward to washing off the bugs in a nice hot shower.

We walk upstairs and quickly realize the fun continues. All over the sheets, pillows, and walls are the same tiny black bugs we became so close with throughout the day. I curse. A lot. We do our best to get the bugs off and close the window opting for heat rather than insects. I am not sure which was worse.

We stomp downstairs and a familiar voice says hello. It is John from New Orleans! His third night staying in the same town as we are and bumping into us randomly.

"How'd ya sleep last night?" he asks, inquiring about the private room he gave us.

"Amazing! Thank you again. You didn't have to do that," I reply. "How bout you?"

"I didn't sleep a wink. Had a couple talented snorers in the room," he laughs. "I am not staying here, though. I got a private room tonight at another place in town. I am here for the food."

We make dinner plans and enjoy a fantastic pilgrim menu with John and some teachers from the United States. I am not as awake as I was last night and find myself remaining quiet and letting others do most of the talking. What a day.

The teachers are on summer break and are approaching the Camino de Santiago as a sort of hop-on, hop-off tour; they hike until they are tired and take a taxi to the next town. Taxis along the Camino are readily available and circle the pilgrims like hungry vultures looking for their next meal. Waiting for a pilgrim to cave to exhaustion before they swoop in and offer a timely ride. A constant temptation for weary pilgrims. I tell myself not to, but I find myself judging the teachers. *How can you grow if you are not challenging yourself physically? That is not the true Camino*, I think to myself, immediately mentally scolding my ego and attempting to change my internal dialogue.

As I am noticeably absent from much of the dinner conversation, my mind drifts back once again to the south of Spain two years earlier. Our Spanish friend Pablo had just given us an incredible gift. Two cream-colored scallop shells painted with a small crimson red cross. I was touched as he explained, "Today all pilgrims carry a scallop shell with them. This is the official mark and symbol of the pilgrim. Carry these on your backpacks during your journey."

Many artistic works during the Middle Ages show St. James with a staff and *concha,* or scallop shell, and the symbol has survived to present day. Pablo explained that the scallop shell is a metaphor. The grooves on the shell all lead to a single point at its base. These grooves represent all of the routes and ways to get to the tomb of St. James in Santiago de Compostela. The waves of the ocean wash scallop shells onto the beaches and shorelines of Galicia. Much as the posted trail markers bearing the scallop shell guide us to Santiago, it is said the very hands of God use the waves to guide the shells to the beach.

I think about this story as I quietly chew my food. I think about the grooves and the many ways to the tomb of St. James. What an amazing metaphor for life and for this journey. How many times have I unconsciously judged someone for doing something I wouldn't? The teachers are forming their own groove in the shell of the Camino. I am forming mine. I glance across the table at Amy who is as silent as I am tonight. She, too, is forming her own path to Santiago even though we walk together.

Upstairs, I lay my head on my pillow, which is covered with a new layer of tiny black bugs. The silence between Amy and me says it all. We are both scared that we will not finish, and it is all because of me. *This can't get worse can it? My body will heal a little right?* Tomorrow we begin again.

Walking Stick

After half falling asleep on a bed of bugs, I am awakened by two late arrivals at one o'clock in the morning. I have no idea how they got in as most albergues lock their doors at around 10 p.m. I gather by their conversation that they are bicycle pilgrims. Yes, you can do this on bikes. They are going the opposite direction on the Camino but are a new item.

When I say "item," I mean I am two seconds away from standing up and tossing them both out of the second story window because they are loudly whispering things like, "I wish we would have met earlier," and "Would you like me to hold you like this?" and on and on. Keep in mind that the occupants of this room are myself, Amy, thousands of little bugs, and these two new love birds. I stand up, storm out of the room, and make a new bed on the couch in the common area of the albergue. At this point, I don't care. I need to sleep, and my earplugs are not working.

I wake up at 5:45 a.m., return to the room, make as much noise as possible to wake up the two love birds whom I am still pissed off at, nudge Amy, and we head out the door. Amy calms me down as we begin to walk, and she reminds me that I am supposed to be loving and accepting of everyone, even horny people who wake me up in the morning. I know she is right. This anger is not serving me at all.

We start heading up a steep hill into thick morning fog, and I can hear the calming whir of giant wind turbines hidden in the gray clouds above our heads. We finally make it to the *Monumento Peregrino*, which marks our high point of the day. We find ourselves in the cold damp embrace of a dark cloud. It is only us up here and a handful of thin, sturdy, metal statues of peregrinos. The figures perfectly posed in the surrounding weather as the wind blows into their metallic faces.

After a short pause to admire these statues, we start our descent. The rocky path proves very difficult as the knee pain of yesterday returns with a vengeance. Amy has forged far ahead, and I have lost sight of her. I have adopted a diagonal method of descent, approaching the trail much like a skier carves out a continuous *S* shape while attacking a steep run.

Many pilgrims pass me on the trail, only pausing to ask me if I am OK. I start to notice my knee looks like I have grown a second kneecap, and I am now almost certain that I will not be able to finish this walk within the 30 days we have planned. The knee brace given to me by the Hungarians yesterday is helping, though, and my breakfast consisted of a 600-mg Spanish ibuprofen. This is helping a little.

I descend from the clouds at a snail's pace. Despite my body, the morning light catching the dew on the expansive golden fields of wheat and the clouds above make Amy and I both pause in awe. For the second time today, we are lost in silence only interrupted now and again by the wind blowing through the wheat. We eventually make our way into the first town for a café con leche and a more substantial breakfast than pain pills.

It is only about 10:00 a.m., and I doubt I can walk much further after that steep descent. As we discuss the possibility of extending the time we have to walk by changing our flights, the Camino provides exactly what I need once again. This trek is trying to teach me to quit worrying.

A group approaches the bar and a very friendly girl with a huge smile walks up to Amy and me and says hello. Her name is Kate, and she is from Seattle. "How is your Camino going?" she asks. I tell her about my knee pain, and she gives me some fantastic advice, "You need a walking stick! Seriously!"

Kate has been walking for weeks already, having started in Le Puy, France, and tells me exactly what I need to hear.

"I cried every day for the first week because the pain was incredible," she explains. "You need to push through the pain of the first week, and it gets better. It always gets better. Your body will find its groove."

She goes on to explain that the walking stick, if used properly, removes 30% of the weight from your legs. Low and behold there are walking sticks for sale at this particular bar. Amy and I thank this stranger for reviving our spirits, buy two walking sticks, and continue on our way.

This stick is amazing! Amy names her stick Alejandro. I name mine Dolores. A girl's name, which I derived from the Spanish word for pain, *dolor*, which seems appropriate. I already feel the difference and the slight relief on my knee. I am filled with hope once again that we may be able to finish! All thanks to Dolores and our angel from Seattle!

As we continue to walk, John from New Orleans catches up to us and yells, "Hey!"

"How are you not hours ahead of us already?" I ask him. "We aren't exactly breaking speed records this morning."

"Slept in and I'm a bit hungover. Too much wine last night!" he replies with a big smile. "Took advantage of that private room. Amazing!"

He immediately notices the new gear, and after I tell him how much it is already helping, he tells me that this is exactly what he needs and decides to buy one in the next town.

"Isn't it weird how the Camino provides exactly what you need right when you need it?" John asks.

I smile and nod, "You have no idea."

We eventually separate again as John's pace is much faster than mine. We take today slowly and stop for snacks in most every village and town. I am leaning heavily on the right leg and noticing something disturbing. My right knee is starting to burn as well.

"How is your knee?" I check in with Amy.

"It still hurts but I think it is getting better," she replies. "Must be all that yoga I was doing before we left! My joints are juicy!"

After only 8 miles total for the day, we sit for yet another rest, planning to continue when a guy named Peter from Ireland sits down to join us for a coffee. Peter has done the Camino de Santiago before and offers some sound advice. He tells us to stop here for the day and take it easy. He reminds us that this is not a race. Yes, part of the Way is suffering but you will be angry if you permanently injure yourself and have to have some sort of procedure when you go home. This is apparently more common than one might think. People get into a sort of crazed zone out here and refuse to stop.

He tells us to remember there are many ways to Santiago. I pluck this advice from the air and chew on it for a while. Incredible food for thought and a life lesson I desperately need to learn. I repeat it over and over again in my head. *There are many ways to Santiago.* This is not a competition. The advice sinks in, and we decide to stop here for the night. There are six or seven albergues in this village, so before deciding on one, we buy a fresh tube of Voltaren, a strong pain cream, from a drug store. I rub the cream into my knee as Amy chooses an albergue from the guidebook.

Despite the conversation with the Irishman, I am still sad and deflated. The feelings of being average race to the front of my mind. In all of my jobs and all of my failed projects, I have always been just "OK"—or at least that is how I've felt. I have never excelled at one particular thing, and this situation is not helping. We may have to take a bus, which will further confirm how average I am.

My mind takes me back decades in an instant. I am a kid exploring a river in the mountains of Colorado. My river. My mom and I lived next to it. In a tent. I didn't know it at the time or really get it, but we were pretty poor. For me, we were camping for a while. Now, of course I understand that we were homeless. People don't normally live in tents. Even temporarily.

My parents were already divorced, and my dad was in prison, serving time for drunk driving. I was too young to understand alcoholism or that my absent father was dealing with his own demons. They both loved me, which was all that mattered. I am lucky in that regard. My mom cleaned houses to make ends meet, and as an only child, I spent a lot of time alone.

As I got a little older, I noticed the cookie cutter houses and the "normal" families. The families that sent their kids to school with Lunchables, drove their kids around in new cars, and parents that were still married, families still whole. I started to play baseball in high school, which made me feel normal. Dad was out of prison and doing better. We spent hours together practicing, pitching, hitting, bonding. I was decent. I thought I was great. I wanted to play professional baseball for the Colorado Rockies. I wanted to excel at everything so the world would know that I was normal. Better than normal. Extraordinary. They would welcome me into their "normal club," and people would admire me. People would read about this kid from a small town while sitting in their fancy houses and they would approve. They would envy me.

Baseball became my obsession. I spent hours practicing, improving and doing everything I could to become better. My dad and I would make the long drive from our small mountain town in Colorado to Denver to watch the Rockies play. I remember looking at the larger than life players, gawking wide-eyed at the immense size of Coors Field and wanting with all of my soul to play on that field someday. My dad wanted this for me, too. I was so focused on this outcome, on this goal, that I started not to enjoy playing the game that I loved. I based my self-worth squarely on baseball.

If I didn't play well, I would feel like the world was ending. I would throw tantrums, hurling bats, balls, and equipment through the air. After a game in which I played particularly bad, I remember a friendly parent telling me, "Good game, Gabe!" to which I replied, "Screw you!" I was so focused on the future, on getting to college ball and the pros that it had ruined the present moment.

My obsession took away from simply enjoying the game, which ironically probably would have made me a better player.

Baseball didn't work out. Failure number one.

"You OK?" Amy asks. She is standing in front of me with her pack on. "Let's go find a place to stay." I realize I am in a competition here on the Camino. A competition with myself.

We check into our chosen albergue, collect another colorful stamp, shower and down a delicious cold sangria which helps to dull the pain. During dinner Amy tries to use her psychology skills to unsuccessfully talk me out of this "average" line of thinking. I am thankful she is here.

The dining hall reminds me of a school cafeteria, and I glance around to see a giant group of French school kids who are staying here for the night. They seem to be on some sort of Camino de Santiago school trip. These kids, who are a bit of an annoyance, end up providing me with a good laugh. As we lie down on our bunks for the night and the lights are turned off, the fun begins.

Our albergue has around 40 beds tightly packed into a giant concrete room. I notice an Italian man stripped down to a tiny green thong, walk past my bunk, and lie directly on the mattress. I know he is Italian because he has a patch of the Italian flag sewn on the outside of his pack. My "Americanness" finds his thong hilarious, and I mentally nickname him The Angry Italian Thong. The school kids were chatty, granted it was only 8:00 p.m., and the Italian man was getting very, very angry. He started huffing and puffing in his bed.

Then I hear a couple of Americans chatting outside of the room. Their voices carry and the entertainment escalates as The Angry Italian Thong gets up from his bed and starts pacing around all of the bunks. He gives the French kids his loudest, "SHHH!" He simply stands there in his tiny thong staring at them ready for a verbal fight. His angry thong walking accelerates as he starts mumbling, "Mama mia!"

He again makes his way past my bunk to the second door and stares at the Americans who continue talking, somehow ignoring the man. He darts behind the door and again lets out a loud

"SHHH!" This goes on for about 15 minutes, and I can't take it. Laughter lightens my mood.

We wake up before dawn. I did not sleep well, yet again, because of the symphony of snoring common to all albergues. It does not help that I am a light sleeper. Before this trip, many people told me that I will get used to the snoring, and I'll be so tired that I'd sleep right through it. I have not found this to be the case at all. I think that advice must have come from people who snore. My most valued purchase before this trip, which I admit Amy had to convince me to buy, was earplugs, but they help only a little.

We begin the day's trek greeted by a clear, cool, crisp summer morning, and my body is feeling better. Yesterday's short hike has really helped me recover, and I mentally thank Peter the Irishman for urging us to take it easy and stop for the day. I begin to really enjoy today's walk. The morning light changes the colors of the wheat fields and bright red poppies almost by the minute. As minutes turn into hours, pink fields fade to golden yellow then to a sea of green. We walk slowly, but it doesn't matter. The Camino de Santiago simplifies everything, and our only job for the day is to put one foot in front of the other. I can tell it is going to be a hot day as I begin to sweat even before breakfast.

Many people come to the Camino for religious reasons, others for personal growth. Most, like me, seem to be searching for inspiration of some kind. All along the path, you begin to see small sayings written by the pilgrims who came before you. Some written on stones with permanent marker and others on guardrails or walls. You can't help but read them and ponder their messages as you walk. Sometimes they really hit home and speak to you, telling you something you needed to hear.

My mind is deep in thought about my next move in life. Worrying about my career. Worrying about how to figure out what my purpose might be. Worrying about worrying. My walking stick lands on a little gem in the path, and a big grin spreads across my sweaty face. Someone has written these words on a stone, "It's about the Way, not about the destination."

Once again, this is exactly what I needed to hear. The Camino de Santiago so far has been a metaphor for life. You focus on getting to Santiago de Compostela with every step you take, to that perfect job, perfect house, perfect whatever, and you forget to enjoy the journey and path that leads you there. I don't cry but I am definitely moved. This message is so simple. Enjoy life. Do that and everything else falls into place.

I seem to have a particular knack for doing the opposite. A special skill in ruining the present moment in pursuit of a distant goal. I think back to my time on the Travel Channel. This was an amazing opportunity to travel the world for free. The show had five hosts, and all of us had a different take on each city that we would visit. My take was food and music, so it was my job to discover the unique foods and music that made each location special. Our season focused on the Pacific Rim, and we traveled through Australia, New Zealand, and parts of Asia.

This was an absolute dream job. When I received the phone call from the show's producers that I had in fact landed the gig, I screamed like a six-year-old girl. I was elated at first but soon my mind took over and started to dream of more, of what this might lead to. I thought that if this went well, I could actually do this for a career. My baseball type obsession creeped in as I became focused on what might be next.

After our first three weeks of filming, we made our way to film episode four in Darwin, Australia. I had worked particularly hard, with the help of the producers, to set up a day with a famous Aboriginal Australian actor. He took me by boat to a beach that was important to his ancestors and, going with the food theme, took me stingray spear fishing.

We waded out into the turquoise waters of the ocean, and I followed his lead, looking for stingrays, ready to chuck my spear if I saw signs of life. He was doing the same. Hours passed, the camera guy stopped filming and eventually, with nothing to show for our efforts, we returned to the beach. Everyone was disappointed, and we scrambled to make something out of the scene.

His friends were invited, and they played the didgeridoo on the beach using the music to tell incredible stories of their people's past. An amazing day. Unfortunately, all I was focused on was how poorly this might play out on TV. I was obsessed with my hosting ability and if I had said the right thing. I asked the editors, producers, and anyone who would listen if I was doing OK. How could I improve? I wanted badly for this to continue and I could see the end of the show drawing near. Again, I was so focused on what was next, using this as a stepping stone to bigger and better things, that I failed to fully experience an incredible secluded beach, with a kind Aboriginal man, sharing incredible music. This continued throughout the filming of the show, four months of anxiety, when I should have just relaxed and enjoyed the incredible ride.

We continue through more small villages, always guided by the yellow arrows and Camino shell tiles that mark the path. The heat is getting almost unbearable as we enter the afternoon hours. These villages become deserted during siesta, and the only people you see are fellow pilgrims. We start to climb a hill, and my left knee begins to burn. Almost as if they are having a conversation, my right knee chimes in with an equally intense pain as I begin to lean more and more heavily on Dolores.

There is no official start date for the Camino de Santiago. You can begin on any day, at any time, 365 days a year. I chose the month of June because of crowds and weather. The most popular time, aka the most crowded trails, is during August.[1] August is also one of the hottest months in this area of Spain, and today's heat makes me glad I didn't choose August.

As we continue to trudge along beneath the midday summer sun, many pilgrims pass and say buen Camino before speeding on. Then a man whom I would only see once says something to me that will stick with me all the way to Santiago de Compostela. He catches up to me on the trail and surveys my slow pace, my sweaty face, my increasingly shaggy beard. He mutters, "Hola, que tal?" *Hi, how's it goin?*

"Bien y tu?" I respond. *Fine and you?*

We agree it is too hot today. He glances ahead and sees a giant patch of shade. "Hay sombra," he says as he looks me in the eyes. *There is shade.*

He glances down at my knee and says, "Siempre hay que ver el positivo." *You always have to see the positive.* He then walks ahead without saying another word. I stop and smile again. The Camino is full of small lessons today.

The end of the day proves to be brutal. My body is incredibly weak, and Estella, our destination, seems like a mirage that will never come. With every step, I feel like the tendon in my right knee will snap, and the heat has swollen my left knee to a disturbing size and shape. The trail is full of small hills, followed by painful descents. Up down, up down, up down. My knee brace keeps slipping to my shin because of the sweat coming out of my pores. The blisters forming on my hands, from leaning on Dolores, are raw and swelling with the heat pulsing through my body. I drag my carcass forward, willing it to carry on. Amy and I don't speak for hours. We simply take a break after every bend in the trail, when our disappointment at not seeing Estella forces us to sit and rest. I feel like our water bottles: empty.

When we finally make it to Estella, I collapse in a chair of the first albergue we see. Absorbed in my own misery, I don't notice the concerned look on the hospitalera's face. Amy does the talking, in Spanish, while I stare at the floor. "She thinks you might die," Amy jokes when the hospitalera leaves to retrieve keys.

"Haha," I sarcastically reply.

"Keep it up, she feels sorry for us so she is giving us a private room for the same price as the bunks in the main room!" she says. "She told me there is no way you could climb into a top bunk!"

"Sadly that is probably true," I reply.

Our private room is more like a cubicle with tall walls which don't quite reach the ceiling. We do have a door which provides some privacy as we are situated in the middle of a giant room full of beds. I am not complaining. The cost is only 5 euro per person, one of our cheapest nights thus far.

After getting settled, we go to the closest restaurant to eat because it is, well, closest. I am surprised by an amazing bowl of *gazpacho*, a cold Spanish tomato soup blended with garlic and vinegar. This followed by a Spanish feast fit for a king. Food always lightens my mood.

"I miss Spain," Amy says between slurps of refreshing soup.

"What do you mean?" I reply. "We are here right now."

"Should we move back? It is so simple here. Good food, good people and a more laid back way of life," she explains, fully aware this will not happen anytime soon for us. "I just miss so much about Spain. Waiters ignore you, you can eat a meal for hours, chain restaurants don't really exist, you don't need a car, siesta, the numerous holidays, Flamenco shows, the cheap wine, Europe being our playground and sunsets overlooking the Alhambra in Granada listening to hippies play the guitar."

"We did that for two years, and it was awesome. Remember how much we missed the States though? The grass is always greener," I slop up the gazpacho with a thick slice of fresh bread. "When you were ahead of me on the trail today, a man told me that you always have to look at the positive. Don't forget how much you love Denver."

"But working 50 and 60 hour weeks is stupid!" Amy continues.

"Don't forget traffic! Oh, how I hate traffic. At least we have jobs," I say, not quite believing myself. "And hey, don't forget how awesome it is that you have the entire summer off!"

Back in the albergue, I rub pain cream on both knees and take more pills. Maybe tonight we will sleep. What an incredible day full of life lessons. This, I think, this is what I came here for. I certainly need to focus less on the hot sun and more on the shade. I can't wait to see what adventures tomorrow brings.

La Rioja

"Here it is!" I yell back to Amy. We both set down our packs to read the sign mounted on a large stone wall.

"¡PEREGRINO! Si quieres llegar a Santiago con fuerza y vitalidad, de este gran vino echa un trago y brinda por la Felicidad." *PILGRIM! If you want to arrive in Santiago with strength and vitality, take a swig of this great wine and toast to happiness.*

"Sounds good to me," Amy walks up to the large fountain. We have arrived at the *Fuente del Vino.* A fountain of wine! Set up by winery *Bodegas Irache,* pulling the handle on *La Fuente* dispenses wine instead of water! As the sign says, pilgrims who drink from the fountain will gain strength that will help them on the Way. We grab a drink. Who cares if it is ten in the morning! I use my small Camino shell as a tiny make shift cup and take a sip of wine.

A sense of hope grows within me today with each step. I feel lucky to not have any new physical issues. Yes, the knees still hurt, but at least they're not getting worse. We continue to meet fascinating people from all walks of life. A couple from Texas who walks parts of the Camino every summer, two Australian guys on their annual worldly adventure, and again we see the burly Austrian Santa Claus. I try to glean small daily life lessons from them all, remembering what The Barista told me a few days ago. Everyone has something to teach you. Many a conversation turn to physical ailments as most pilgrims have something wrong with their bodies.

I have noticed that most are struggling with blisters. Some with over a dozen blisters between their two feet. I sit and watch a pilgrim poke a particularly bulbous blister with a needle and gingerly pull a line of thread through. "So it can drain," she says. I wince with her in pain as she continues her treatment.

I think of the man we saw on our first day, walking barefoot and wonder how his feet are doing. This pilgrim is wearing sturdy hiking boots, and I have started to notice a trend. Hiking boots equal blisters. I elected trail running shoes over the less flexible hiking boots and am beginning to think I made the right decision. So far my blister count is zero, and I have soft city boy feet. Apart from Amy's blister on the first day, she has had no new blisters thus far.

Back on the trail we meet an incredibly nice man from Spain named Pepe. Walking with us for a while, he explains the customs and food of his region of Spain. He is from Tarragona and is in his mid 40s. When asked why he is here, he tells us, "To find peace."

He is single and feels it may be too late to meet "the one." His voice saddened by this thought. This is something that lately has been filling him with a lot of anxiety.

"You never know," I say trying to cheer him up, "Today could be the day!" I tell him the story of how Amy and I met. It was nearly eight years ago in a coffee shop in Colorado. When I saw her, I told the friend who introduced us, "I will marry that girl someday," and I meant it. A few minutes on a random day changed the course of both our lives.

"Today could be the day," I repeat. We eventually separate as I am walking far too slowly for his pace, and we say our goodbyes.

We are alone again. The fields of wheat surround the trail in nearly every direction as far as the eye can see. Giant gusts of wind skim the tops of the fields, reminding me of sitting on a beach watching the ocean ebb and flow. The scene is spectacular as each individual plant bends in unison as if guided by an invisible hand.

We make our way to Los Arcos by late afternoon and decide to splurge on a private room. I do feel a pang of guilt for electing a private room and feel like maybe we are missing out or cheating the experience in some way. I soon get over that notion as we enter our room. Oh, the luxury! Towels, a bed, a private shower, electric outlets, internet, and most importantly, total silence! I can leave the earplugs in the pack tonight. After a shower and an afternoon nap, we scan this tiny quaint town for a pilgrim menu and some much needed calories.

We dine in an old Spanish plaza surrounded by kids playing soccer and hungry pilgrims devouring fish, fried potatoes and *lomo,* a Spanish pork dish. We wash down the food with a fresh pitcher of sangria and sit to take in the scene.

A large group of pilgrims speaking Portuguese sits to our right enjoying giant steaming bowls of soup. A young pilgrim in his early 20s from Belgium sits at a table to our left with a few guys from Australia. They are stuffing their packs with bottles of Rioja wine, bread, Manchego cheese, and Spanish *Jamón,* or cured ham. They have decided to continue on and find a place to sleep in a field somewhere under the stars. The tired pilgrims contrast with well-dressed locals who stream into the cathedral in the square. They look so clean in their Sunday best. The scene is so European, so perfect, and so wonderfully unique.

"Have a good night, guys," the young Belgian says as his group gets up to leave.

We wave goodbye as they walk out of town into the twilight, in search of the perfect campsite.

Chances are that if you drink wine, you have heard of the Rioja region of Spain. Here they produce world-renowned red wines aged in oak barrels that help them develop their trademark vanilla notes. They have been making wine here since medieval times, and I know many a pilgrim before me has indulged in the deep crimson liquid gold while passing through La Rioja.

"I wonder if those guys who were going to sleep in a field last night slept here," I say to Amy pointing at a large open field. There is an empty bottle of Rioja wine and evidence of a makeshift fire pit. It is almost noon on our seventh day on the trail.

Today we cross from the region of Navarre into La Rioja, and after a 17-mile walk, I am looking forward to a foodie's dinner fit for a Spanish king. We follow the yellow arrows of the Camino that are becoming a constant comfort guiding us through Spain. My mantra for the day is simply, "Enjoy yourself," which I repeat as we walk through the fields.

We are behind schedule if we are going to make it to Santiago de Compostela in 30 days. But today I decide to try and stop acting like a crazed marathon athlete set on breaking a world record. I try to remember the point of this trip. It is about personal growth, not competing with the other people on the trail. I see a quote in our guidebook that resonates: *We are speeding up our lives and working harder, in a futile attempt to slow down and enjoy it.* —Paul Hawken

Taking Mr. Hawken's advice, we decide to take a break at a small bar in the heart of a charming little Spanish village. We grab a seat outside to enjoy some sun, and at the table next to us is the first interesting person of the day. An artist from California who has been keeping a journal of her trek via paintings. She looks to be in her mid 50s, and she reveals herself to be an eccentric soul as she shows us her art. I am blown away by her talent.

We slowly savor an afternoon café con leche as she tells us that she is also keeping a blog about her Camino. In fact, the majority of the Americans we have met so far have told me the same. I am keeping a blog, too. Does this say something about our American culture? I am starting to feel like a blogging American cliché. We say our goodbyes as she is planning on taking a taxi today. She invites us to come along and I politely decline. I catch myself judging her despite my best efforts. Just like I did to the teachers a few days ago. A taxi. How could she? Again, I think of the shell strapped to my backpack. There are many ways to Santiago.

We near the border of Navarre and La Rioja and find ourselves in the middle of nowhere. There is not a building in site. We soon hit a sheep traffic jam, and I grab my iPhone to capture the scene. A shepherd guides his flock towards us, and as we make room for them to pass, I feel as if we are walking upstream through white puffy water. The bells on their necks call out constantly. I smile at the shepherd and wave hello. He does not wave or smile back. He has the frown of a man doing work he does not enjoy. I recognize it all too well.

The wind picks up, and the fields of wheat are gone. It is bone dry out here and tumbleweeds roll by, speeding through the dust to their own destinations. Up ahead I spot a small van, and a man starts to yell at us through a megaphone.

"Bienvenidos a La Rioja, peregrinos!" he screams kicking up dust with excitement. *Welcome to La Rioja, pilgrims.*

It's a ridiculous scene. Two American pilgrims, in the middle of nowhere, looking on in bewilderment, maybe a bit of embarrassment, as a man stands in front of his van drowning out an invisible crowd with his megaphone. As we near, he continues to yell but I am too tired to translate from Spanish. He is selling snacks and water. We politely decline and continue on our way.

The afternoon is hot, and we are dead tired as we near Logroño. The scenery turns increasingly ugly. The smooth dirt path turns into cracked paved roads as we pass crumbling buildings covered in graffiti. This makes the last part of the day seem especially long as we just focus on putting one foot in front of the other. The black pavement seems to amplify the heat. By about 4 p.m., our feet drag us into town, and we check into an albergue.

The room is clean but packed with 15 rows of bunks. The door swings open and in walks a rowdy group of 15 bicycle pilgrims. I am feeling claustrophobic, so we quickly wash off the day's muck and head out to eat. Logroño is the capital of La Rioja, and my expectations are high for a great meal with great wine.

We head to a place called *Café Moderno* and have a fantastic pilgrim menu for 9 euro. Our waiter is rude, which is a good sign. During my two years living in Spain, I have learned if your waiter is nice to you, then there is a good chance that you have fallen into a tourist trap.

The meal starts with some pickled asparagus drenched in olive oil and vinegar. Delicious! This is followed by *bacalao,* salted white fish, smothered in a delicious red pepper sauce, which we wash down with a bottle of red wine. For dessert, homemade *flan.* A creamy, gelatinous, sweet glob of goodness, flan is arguably the national dessert of Spain and found on almost every menu.

The café is filled with senior citizens playing some kind of card game at the tables. They make their moves in between sips of wine and seem to be right at home yelling at each other in protest when the cards don't go their way. The waiters speed around the large café, yelling out orders with frowns on their faces. A wonderful scene.

The wine is delicious and is having the right amount of numbing effect on my tired feet. Not quite ready for bed, Amy and I decide to head to a wine bar to sample some *Crianza.* Crianza is basically a step up from the house reds or the basic cheap bottles you get everywhere. It spends a year in oak and at least a year in the bottle before being served.

Dear God, the glasses of wine are glorious. We get the bill, and my head spins. Only 1.20 euro a glass! By American standards, that is one cheap glass of wine. Another reason I love Spain.

Over our amazing glasses of wine, Amy and I start to recalculate the rest of our walk and new hope rises in us both. We scan our map and guidebook, crunching the numbers and relishing in the mathematical good news. If I can maintain our pace without new injuries and deal with the current knee pain, then we actually may be able to finish within our planned 30-day time frame. A couple of 30-kilometer days stand in our way but there is hope! Amy lifts her glass. "A toast," she says with a glimmer in her eye. "To finding the joy in everything. To feeling inspired. To hope."

"And to cheap wine that tastes expensive!" I reply.

With new optimism still fresh in my mind, I wake up at 5 a.m. and groggily look around. The cyclists are still snug in their beds snoring like a herd of dying sheep. We head outside and walk through the dark morning before sunrise. The cobblestone streets of Logroño are empty, and the only sound is the constant tap tap tap of our walking sticks and the echo off the buildings in reply. The streets are wet from overnight rain, and the air smells earthy, full of life, clean, and delicious. I have noticed that on the Camino, your body can either wake up ready to go or just simply resist your every attempt at moving forward. Today, both Amy and I are dragging. Every step is a focused effort, and I am a little hungover from last night's wine.

We barely speak as we make our way outside of the city. The sun slowly peeks its head above the horizon, and the morning cold starts to fade away. We climb hills filled with miles and miles of vineyards as far as the eye can see. The signature red clay of this region shines bright under the old vines, which produce the region's wines. It is a spectacular view. A spectacular sunrise.

I decide on no mantra for the day. No phrase to focus on. I am just trying not to think as I am starting to drive myself a little crazy. I am again looking for a bright flashing sign with the lesson I am supposed to take away from this trip and trying to think about my purpose. I have never been focused on a life plan or had a steady career path, and it has always been a sour spot in life. Always that thorn in my side. I have a college degree, and I like the jobs that I have had—some I have even loved—but over time, that has faded into boredom. Either that, or I ruin everything by worrying about what might be next.

Maybe this is a side effect of the incessant travel bug I can never shake and my constant search for something new and exciting. Amy is lucky. She has been passionate about her job as a school psychologist up to this point and has always had that clear direction. On top of that, she has plans to get her yoga teacher certification when we return. Two passions for her, not even one for me.

Today, the neon sign doesn't come for me. We continue to see familiar faces now and again as we walk and take breaks for food, water, and coffee. But for the most part we are alone as we trudge along through the beautiful sea of vines. I express to Amy my all too familiar frustration and as always, she guides me to a new line of thinking. She begins to ask me a series of questions.

"What are you feeling right now?" she asks.

"Anxiety. Fear. Frustration," I reply.

"Why?" she asks.

"Because I have spent 10 years trying to figure out what my passion is in life and what I should be doing for a career, and here I am still without an answer," I say. Two pilgrims on their bikes whiz past us on the trail. The psychological line of questioning continues.

"Many people spend their lives trying to find that perfect job. I want to know *why* it matters so much to you. Why does it give you so much anxiety and that feeling of restlessness?" Amy pushes.

I think about this for a while limping forward and tightly clutching Dolores. "Because I guess ... I guess I want to matter. I want my life to have mattered." I fight back tears as we walk.

Amy continues to pry, "So your life doesn't matter now? Because you don't have a flashy career? Because you don't make huge sums of money?" She drives home her point and lets me think about it before continuing. I let it sink in.

"I know. I know. I just want to do something special. Something meaningful. Like you. Like so many of our friends," I say.

"Don't you think it is funny how you want to be so different from everyone? So special. But at the same time you want to be just like everyone else," she wisely replies. "Now what can you do about it? What are actions you can take to get to a place you want to be? Or at least find peace with where you are now." That is a fantastic question. One I don't have the answer to just yet. My mind takes me into my past, looking for the answer.

It is 1999. I am a junior in high school. My nickname on the baseball team is *brown eye*. I was born with a dark brown birthmark, the size of a dime, directly under my right eye. Every time I meet someone new they ask me the same question, "What happened to your eye?" I normally make a joke along the lines of, *You should have seen the other guy*, but I have become obsessed with this one physical feature. I want it gone. It definitely does not help me feel normal.

By college, the birthmark is the only thing I can see when I look in the mirror. Well-meaning friends and family tell me that it is unique. It makes me who I am. I think it looks like a permanent black eye and will ensure I will die alone with 10 cats. I desperately want to look like everybody else. Eventually I go through a series of expensive laser treatments to have it removed. With each treatment a metal contact lens is shoved into my eye to protect it from the laser. Then the skin is blasted with an intense beam. This is the easy part. For weeks after the treatment, my eye is red, puffy, and oozing blood. I avoid people at all costs until a blister forms and falls off leaving the birthmark a few shades lighter than before. This takes years, and costs thousands of dollars. It works, and I feel normal. No one asks me what happened to my eye anymore. My confidence grows.

We come to a high point with sweeping views of Logroño behind us and a busy highway below. I notice woven into the chain link fence beside the trail are hundreds upon hundreds of tiny crosses that pilgrims have weaved into the twisted wires of the fence. They use string, twigs, plastic, weeds, or anything that can be used as a makeshift cross.

The pilgrim's office in Santiago keeps detailed statistics every year about the Camino de Santiago. When you get to the office to claim your compostela, they will ask you to check one of three boxes that defines your reason for walking to Santiago. In 2013, 39.97% of the pilgrims who walked the Camino de Santiago did so for "religious purposes." Like me, 54.56% took on the challenge for "spiritual, cultural or other reasons." Only 5.47% checked the box for "no religious motivation."[1] The tiny crosses left here by the "religious purposes" group go on for a mile or so entwined into the long fence. An incredible sight.

The pain in my left knee is still a constant companion and starts to swell again as the hours pass. I know they mean well, but I start resenting every person who passes me, young and old, asking if I am going to be alright and then giving me their opinion about how unlikely it is I will be able to finish. I am still focused on one step at a time as we slowly close in on a colossal 30-kilometer day. The last hour of every day is always the hardest, and we finally make it to Nájera for the night. We again decide to splurge on a private room.

Nájera is a small historic pilgrim town. With a population of about 7,000, it has a long history with the Camino de Santiago.[2] Cathedrals in town contain pilgrim works of art, and Roman artifacts can be found in the local museum. Like many towns on the Camino de Santiago, pilgrims provide a huge boost to the local economy. Sometimes the only source of income and the main industry in town. Unfortunately, every single step counts, so I will be seeing none of the artifacts here. If it is not directly on the path, we will miss it. We are on a budget, too, and have to watch our extra spending money. So far we have spent about 35 euro per person per day, which is starting to add up. A bed at an albergue normally costs about 9 euro per person. A private room costs about 20 euro per person. Food has been about 22 euro per person each day. Our budget is 1,000 euro per person for the entire trip, which works out to roughly 33 euro a day.

After sitting through dinner, my body clenches up around itself, and when I try to move again it creaks and aches and screams, "NO!" We shall see how far we get tomorrow. I had no idea how physically challenging the Camino de Santiago was going to be.

Camino Surprises

Trail Days 9—10

The day begins with the ninth sunrise seen in nine days. Little did I know what amazing things today would hold. The Camino de Santiago is full of surprises. Soon the orange rays of the sun peek above the hills, and the Way is illuminated. The soreness of yesterday's walk gingerly melts into today's new and fresh pain.

Slowly the miles of vineyards get left behind and turn into fields of sea green wheat spotted with bright orange and red poppies. My stomach growls. Time for breakfast. We stop at a bar and sit with other pilgrims who are hungrily scarfing down *tortilla española,* or Spanish potato omelette, fresh squeezed orange juice and café con leche. I spot our new friend Pepe from Tarragona who pulls up a chair at our table.

I am beginning to grow quite fond of Pepe, and today he tells us about the *castells* from his region within Catalonia, Spain. He whips out his camera and shows us pictures of these human towers that are built during festivals in his hometown. Pepe is such a kind soul, and I love how proud he is of his culture.

"Did you meet your future wife yet?" I ask jokingly, recalling our conversation from a few days ago.

"Not yet!" he replies. "Not yet."

The day passes, and I am starting to feel like I am physically improving. The knee pain is tolerable even though it seems a new part of my body hurts every day. The limbs take turns, and today my right Achilles' heel begins to ache. We make it to our destination for the day, Grañon, without further issues.

This sleepy little village exists because of the Camino de Santiago. We enter the town, passing some pilgrims with a donkey carrying their packs and decide to stay in a *donativo*. Simply meaning, you donate what you can afford for the night. There is no set price.

The donativo is part of The Church of Saint John the Baptist, which has an albergue attached. We make our way through an old door marked only with a brass Camino shell knocker. Immediately this place has a great sense of history as we head up an old stone stairway. It feels as if we have entered a castle, and we are greeted by a friendly hospitalero as we take off our shoes and survey the room.

It appears that we will be sleeping on the floor tonight as we are given two thin brown mats and, imitating those already there, we pick a spot in the corner to make our beds. I know I won't be sleeping much tonight. We are informed that there is a pilgrim's mass being held in the adjacent church and decide to check it out. I am not Catholic but am open to the spirituality of the experience, and we limp into an empty pew. An opportunity for silence. A time for thought.

I have definitely prayed for purpose before. Quitting jobs where everything seems right on the outside but everything seems wrong in your soul is a hard thing to do. During these times, I have prayed. Growing up, my church was nature. My mom would drag me into the woods, find a tree, and make me sit in silence. She would tell me that this is where you will find God. This is where you should pray. I hated it at the time, but nature is still the place I feel closest to something more, something out of this world, something spiritual. I pray now, here in this small church, in the middle of nowhere in Spain. *Why am I here? What am I meant to do?*

I often wonder if I want too much out of life. Does anybody really love their job? Does the perfect job even exist? I think about my current job back in the United States. It is OK. I work for a non-profit, which provides me with a small sense of purpose. Most days I feel like a replaceable cog in a giant wheel. But the job is neither good nor bad. I have had worse, and I have had better. I send up another prayer in hopes that somebody is listening. *Should I be happy with good enough? If so, please help me feel content.*

Pilgrims are intermixed with a handful of locals, most of whom appear to be in their 80s. I glance around the small but beautiful church. Many of the stained glass windows in the walls have images of pilgrims and the symbolic scallop shells of the Camino de Santiago. The deep colors lit by the late afternoon Spanish sun. The service is quite moving as the priest eventually brings all of the pilgrims to the front, places his hands on our little circle, and says a prayer for us all. Wishing us a buen Camino and safe arrival to Santiago. It really is quite powerful as I think of the thousands who have stood in this very spot over the centuries.

After mass, our stomachs lead us back to the albergue for an amazing feast that we are told is paid for by the previous night's donations! The room is full of pilgrims dining communal style, swapping stories, and making new international friends. I make friends with a man sitting beside me named Tom.

Tom is bald with a silvery goatee and a sunburned face. He is slightly overweight and has gentle, kind, gray eyes. We start with the polite details of life. I learn that he is retired, is from the United States, but currently calls France home. As we talk about our motivation for this journey, he suddenly opens up and tells me his reason for walking. I feel a flash of shame as I think about my stupid petty problems.

He and his 30-year-old daughter had traveled together while on vacation a few years ago in Spain. During their trip, they spotted some people walking the Camino de Santiago and made plans to do it together someday. They agreed it could be an amazing father and daughter bonding experience. His daughter returned home, and only a few months after making plans with her father, took her own life.

"A suicide I did not see coming. I can't understand why. The why. That is what is haunting me," Tom says, the words tumbling out from somewhere deep inside him.

I don't know what to say as the people around us continue to talk and eat their food. Tears try to fight their way out, but he successfully holds them at bay. What an incredible amount of pain he must be carrying with him as he walks. He is suffering a pain far greater than any physical ailment any of us in the room have experienced thus far.

I simply stare at my plate and poke my food. I make lame attempts at finding words of comfort as so many do when they hear something so raw.

"This is my second Camino. I plan to walk each year until I no longer am able," his voice cracks as he looks down at his plate, still fighting back tears. I put my hand on his shoulder and say the only thing that comes to mind, "I am so sorry." The words are inadequate. I truly hope he finds peace through this journey.

After dinner, we all pitch in cleaning up and giving a donation so that tomorrow's pilgrims can also enjoy a good meal. The night does not end as all of us are invited to a group meditation in the back of the church. I feel like Indiana Jones as we slip through a small hidden door and find our seats in giant black carved wooden chairs in the back of the church. The dim room is lit only by candles. Amy and I are wide eyed and don't quite know what to expect. I look around the room and through the candlelight see six or seven other pilgrims who have settled into their seats.

The hospitalero quiets everyone and speaks softly, holding a candle to his face. "Why are you here, peregrinos?" He slowly repeats the question as he scans the room, "Why ... are ... you ... here?"

We are asked to think about our reasons for walking the Camino de Santiago, and we all do so in silence. Then, one by one, the candle is passed around the room, and we can either share our reasons out loud with the group or simply keep it to ourselves. I keep my mouth closed and pass it along. I feel foolish now after hearing Tom's story. What do I have to complain about? The silence is golden.

We sit in silent candlelight in meditation and reflection for a while before being led down into the church as the hospitalero points out carved figures and stained glass renditions of the Camino shell. Experiencing this level of intimate history is incredible.

After this amazing session, I feel spiritually refreshed and physically exhausted. My body still hurts as I fall to my mat on the floor back in the albergue. Another surprise awaits. A man from Portugal, a complete stranger, gestures for me to stay still and begins massaging my aching legs with olive oil! He is part of a larger group from Brazil that we have seen walking together for the past few days. He knows what he is doing as his skilled rough hands try to loosen my tired tendons and muscles. It hurts, a lot, but I trust him not to break me.

At first I am a bit nervous. This is a bit weird, right? Getting a massage from a stranger? I glance at Amy who is bewildered, too, her big brown eyes wide in stunned observation. A few other pilgrims have whipped out their cameras and start to take pictures. As he works, I am overcome with complete gratitude at such a kind act. I know he is tired, too, and he is asking nothing in return. He does not know me. Pure kindness. I am blown away as he spends 15 minutes rubbing my legs. He doesn't speak English, and I just smile, clasping my hands to my chest and say thank you over and over again.

This has been an absolutely incredible night. I resolve to be like this man and spread random acts of kindness. That is what life is all about. I honestly can't remember the last time I did something nice for a complete stranger. So caught up in my own life and too busy to give someone I don't know a second glance. Sleep doesn't come as I am a buzz with thoughts of the day. I promise my future self that I will work to be more kind. The lights are shut off at 10 p.m., and the familiar chorus of snores slowly rises and echoes off the walls. But who cares? This is the stuff of adventure!

In the morning, my legs do feel a little bit better thanks to my impromptu massage. It is 4:45 a.m., and I am still buzzing from last night. I am surprised to see that most of the room in the albergue is empty. The group of Brazilians and the Portuguese man who massaged my legs are all gone. They got an early start. I peel myself off the floor. My back creaks and pops. It hurts from using my backpack as a pillow.

From the get go early this morning, we are focusing on physically moving forward as after a few hours my knee pain returns with a vengeance, absolutely screaming with every step. It has begun to collapse without warning.

As I walk, if I step slightly wrong, it will simply give out, and I have to catch myself with my walking stick. Sometimes almost falling to the ground. This is not a good sign, and I know the fact that I no longer use the leg normally can't be good. I am trying not to support my weight with my knee and keep it as straight as possible when going up or down a hill. If I don't, a shock of electric pain causes an immediate uncontrollable protest. I think over and over again, *Should I stop? Is this the sign of a permanent injury?*

The serene Spanish morning unfolds as the typical early hour chill quickly gives way to intense sunshine and heat. I am entering a sort of delirium and after a few hours decide to listen to music for the first time for some motivation. I cue up my iPhone with some upbeat tunes and look around. We truly are in the middle of nowhere.

The wind is spectacular today as it blows over the wheat fields, magically making waves appear on land. The music acts as a sort of real life movie soundtrack. Hours pass, putting one foot in front of the other as one wheat field slowly melts into the next. We finally make it to a side of the road, hole in the wall bar and stop for sustenance. We sit down as flies scatter from our table.

I am in a lot of pain and for the first time vocalize to Amy, "This is bullshit! Let's quit, take a bus to Granada and eat tapas for the rest of our time in Spain. Why are we doing this to ourselves?"

She smiles and takes a picture of me instead of responding to my little fit. She shows the picture to me and says, "Stop taking yourself so seriously."

I look pitiful. Toothpaste drippings stain my shirt right above the right nipple. The sweat of the day has matted my hair like a feral cat's coat. Every hair of my beard seems to point in a different direction. I am not in the mood for a life lesson from Amy, so I don't respond. She laughs, though, and focuses on the food. I am feeling down, and my spirits are low.

After a *bocadillo de Jamón*, cured Spanish ham sandwich, we continue on. I have begun to notice memorials along the trail for the many pilgrims who have died on the Camino de Santiago. Unfortunately, every year a few pilgrims do die out here. Some years are more brutal than others. The memorials range from pictures fastened to trees to small stone monuments with messages from loved ones. The Spanish Federation website keeps a list of those who have died and the causes range from being hit by vehicles, having a heart attack, or even getting caught in a snow storm while crossing the Pyrenees and dying of hypothermia. A total of nine people died while trying to complete the Camino de Santiago in 2013.[1]

I have been thinking about death a lot lately. Maybe it's because of the underlying issue that Amy was able to pin down a few days ago. How do you make your life matter before you are gone? I really want to know. Maybe I am a bit too introspective for my own good, but I can't help it. What happens after we die? What is the point? I think about Tom from last night's dinner. Where is his daughter now?

St. James seems to have gained some sort of immortality. People have been walking in his name for thousands of years. But is that the kind of life that really matters? I have to admit that as a pilgrim, I don't care much about St. James. The stories about him appearing on a battlefield hundreds of years after his death to lop off the heads of Islamic soldiers seem like a bit of a stretch. It also seems sort of wrong that we are celebrating this kind of violent story. As my mind has a vigorous debate and conversation with itself, the Camino gives me my answer.

Amy is far ahead as I am making very slow progress up a hill. I take off my headphones for a second as I watch the wind blow waves over the fields. I pass a woman filming the ground with her phone. She yells to the camera as she is alone, "See! Look!"

I look at the ground as I pass, and someone has spelled out in small purple and white flowers, "Enjoy yourself while you are here."

A smile spreads across my face. "Thank you," I say to no one in particular and continue on my way. This moment is all that matters and is truly all we have. I think about a quote by G.K. Chesterton that fits this situation perfectly: "Happiness is a mystery, like religion, and should never be rationalized."

After eight hours, we eventually make it to our destination. We decide on a private room for a total of 36 euro including breakfast. I want to sleep tonight, so the wall is key. We head downstairs to grab a snack and run into our Brazilian friends and the Portuguese massage man from last night who are staying at the same place.

"Hello!" I say to the massage man. I am happy to see him again.

"Olá," he replies in Portuguese and points to my legs to ask how I am doing.

"Not good," I frown. I point to the swollen part of my kneecap, and he makes massage gestures, asking if I need another treatment. "Maybe later," I smile, patting him on the shoulder. He looks very concerned, which worries me more. He doesn't like the look of my leg at all.

No one speaks any English or Spanish, so we communicate through gestures and hilarious tones. I am able to get his name, Eloi, and get a better look at him than I did last night. Eloi wears a black beret that makes him look French. He is a shorter man with a snow-white beard and kind blue eyes. I guesstimate him to be in his late 60s, and he has the muscular build of someone who has spent a lifetime working outside.

Eloi is putting his fingers to his lips and rubbing his belly. The international symbol for an invite to dinner. Both Amy and I are introverts and love not being around people sometimes, so we debate with each other until we finally accept. I am so glad we did!

Eloi skillfully prepares the food in the common area kitchen. We enjoy an amazing meal of home cooked soup, cheese, and bread. Because of the language barrier, I have no idea what anyone is saying, but somehow I still feel like we are making new friends. It's amazing how much you can communicate through gestures.

I learn that Eloi has olive trees back home in Portugal. He whips out a tiny green plastic bottle with no label, which I recognize as the oil he used on my legs last night. He pours it on our salads. The homemade olive oil is liquid gold. Absolutely delicious! One of our new Brazilian friends unpacks a guitar during dinner and starts playing some tunes.

Music, the only true universal language. We all sit sipping Spanish wine, eating Portuguese soup, speaking three languages and listening to the man sing relaxing songs while his skillful fingers play the guitar. Everyone content to just listen, think, eat, and relax. I think again about the flowers that spelled out my lesson for the day on the trail, "Enjoy yourself while you are here."

We head off to bed after this fantastic meal with new friends. The soundtrack of the evening playing over and over again in my head. I can't even lie on my chest in bed because it makes my knees hurt. The swelling is bad, and the dinner was a welcome distraction. We have a challenging climb ahead of us tomorrow through an immense oak forest. I hope my body is up to the challenge. Before falling asleep, I glance at some bug bites on my hand. They are neat and tidy little red bumps, all in a row. A shock of recognition hits me. I think I have been bitten by bed bugs.

Bed Bugs

"We are running out of money," Amy says as she checks on our funds in a hidden backpack pocket.

"We haven't seen an ATM for days. The guidebook lies," I reply. I am a bit worried. Credit cards don't get you very far out here. We need cash.

"We can eat unripe blackberries. At least those are free," Amy jokes, pointing to the rows of blackberry bushes that line the trail.

The last 30 hours have passed in a slow walking blur. It is midafternoon on day 12, and I can feel the miles we have completed as we make our way towards Burgos. My body groans and creaks like a rusty old truck as it sputters forward, step-by-step. We have walked so far but have a huge chunk of land still ahead of us.

We make our way through a dense oak forest. Welcome shade covers the trail during the hot afternoon sun. A section of the Camino that in the 16th century was notorious for bandits and robbers who would steal pilgrims' possessions and quickly disappear back into the forest.[1] As I walk, a pilgrim catches up with me and starts walking at my pace beside me.

I recognize him immediately. It is Peter the Irishman, who gave me sound advice to take it easy a few days ago. "Hey! How ya doin?" I enthusiastically greet him.

"Pretty good tanks," he replies in a thick Irish accent. "How's the knee?"

We have some great conversation, which makes the walk speed by. He is a teacher and has done the Camino de Santiago before, during the winter months, which he does not recommend.

"During the winter, your clothes never dry, and your bones are never warm," he explains. "I have never smelled so bad in my life! The clothes develop a sort of musty sweat odor that you can't shake."

"So why are you here again?" I ask. "Glutton for punishment?"

"Just for the adventure. I love the adventure of it out here. It is also a cheap way to spend my summer break and meet lots of interesting people," he replies. "And sometimes you just need a break from real life ya know. It will be my 40th birthday soon, and I am freaking out a little."

Eventually we separate, and say our temporary goodbyes. If the first 12 days are any indication, I know we are likely to see him again. My back is itching, a lot, so when we stop for a snack at a café in a small village I visit the restroom and take off my shirt to see why.

"Shit!" I blurt out in disgust and surprise. What I see on my skin is disturbing and a confirmation of one of the most dreaded enemies of the Camino de Santiago. I have a bed bug problem. My back and hand have the telltale bites of these little pests. If you see three bug bites in a neat little row, chances are these devils have eaten breakfast, lunch, and dinner, as they say. They look like mosquito bites but the bite pattern gives them away as they criss cross the tops of my shoulders in uniform.

Unfortunately, bed bugs are a growing problem on the Camino de Santiago. Due to the bed bug's ability to hitchhike and the transient nature of the Camino, they are spreading quickly. These small, reddish brown oval insects have flat bodies that, like mosquitos, live on the blood of animals. They cannot fly like mosquitos, but they do feed by sucking blood. They are most likely hitching a ride in my sleeping bag, and I probably picked them up somewhere along the Way from a mattress. I have no way of knowing for sure where I got them. Bed bugs come out at night to feed on any exposed areas of skin while you are sleeping.[2]

Back in the café, I tell Amy the bad news, and she decides to go check herself as well. She returns and shares good news. She is bed bug bite free.

We make a quick decision that we should book a nice hotel in Burgos using hotel rewards points and take care of the problem. Using the internet at the café, we learn that the solution is to strip down to nothing and put everything we own in a scalding hot wash, then dry everything in a big dryer at the hottest temperature possible. Bed bugs are extremely sensitive to heat, and this is the only way to kill them.[3] Burgos is a big city, so we think that our chances of finding somewhere to do laundry are good. Even better if the hotel has a laundry service where they can scorch the little bastards that have hitched a ride in my pack.

We slowly make our way into Burgos, and I don't like what I see. Everything is closed. It is not siesta. It is not Sunday. The city should be bustling at this hour. We stop someone on the street, and they confirm my fears: Today is a local Spanish holiday. In Spain that means that nothing will be open for business, especially a laundromat. Our only hope is the swanky hotel we booked. Surely they will cater to my bed bug ridden, panicking American state.

A *Spain Day* is something we experienced every once in a while during our time living in Spain. It basically describes a day when you miss the convenience of the 24-hour American culture. I envy the Spanish culture for its laid back approach to life. They have perfected the art of working to live, not living to work. But for someone who grew up in the American culture of capitalistic convenience, this can be incredibly annoying. This was part of our culture shock when we first moved to Spain. For example, if you want to buy something during the afternoon siesta, good luck, everything is closed!

As we near the hotel, Amy and I debate whether or not we should mention the bed bugs.

"We should probably tell them right?" Amy asks.

"I guess," I reply. "But what if they turn us away?" My conscience is not quite as guilty as Amy's.

"Internet etiquette says that the best thing to do is to tell the hotel so they can take appropriate precautions," Amy argues.

"I don't care what some blogger says about travel etiquette!" I counter. "The internet doesn't have to walk around town looking for a new hotel if they turn us away!"

In the end, I win, and we decide not to tell them why it is imperative we get our laundry done today. We already look homeless, and telling them that I am also carrying bed bugs will not help. Automatic glass doors slide open welcoming us into the well-decorated modern lobby. I can't help but feel like a criminal with a giant secret.

I casually tell the front desk clerk that we would like to do some laundry. She politely explains to us what I already know. It is a local holiday so this might not be possible, but she will check.

"A wonderful holiday! Only here in Burgos!" she explains with a chipper smile. "You are visiting at the perfect time!"

I want to reach into my bag, grab a bed bug, and drop it on her head. She picks up the phone to check on laundry and her look of disappointment says it all. We are screwed. She politely tells me that the company they hire to do guest laundry is on holiday today as well. Sure enough, we are having a *Spain Day*.

Upstairs, we enter our room. A luxurious space greets us with modern decorations, a large glorious bed, a flat screen television, and our first break. There is a tub! Time for plan B. I immediately strip down to nothing and throw everything into the tub, which I fill with scorching hot water. I let it soak for two hours all the while keeping the water as hot as possible. I carefully stir the pot of infested clothes with a hanger from the closet. To finish the killing, I use the hairdryer to dry every inch of every article by hand. I have high hopes that this will work.

There are times in life when you find yourself thinking, *How in the hell did I get to this point in my life?* Drying everything you own with a hairdryer while buck-naked in a fancy hotel is one of those times. I can't help but laugh at the ridiculous hilarity of the situation. After I am finally finished with my attempted extermination, Amy and I decide to go check out Burgos. I wave politely to the front desk lady on the way out the door, concealing my criminal secret.

Burgos is one of the bigger cities along the Camino de Santiago and boasts a population of about 175,000 people.[4] The city is filled with amazing architecture, monuments, and more importantly, some amazing *pintxos*. The scene in Burgos is festive, as most families are out enjoying the day. They are leisurely strolling through the streets and admiring the impressive Gothic architecture of the Burgos cathedral. A UNESCO world heritage site, construction on the cathedral began in 1221, and the sheer size of the beautiful building causes everyone to stop and stare.[5] Rain begins to fall as we drink in the view. We decide we have walked enough and take cover in a tiny restaurant next to the giant cathedral.

Pintxos are similar to the famous *tapas* of southern Spain but smaller and fancier. It is like the difference between a burger and a gourmet burger. Chefs carefully craft small bite size snacks using impressive flavor combinations that force you to eat slowly to savor the flavor. Most creations look like a small work of art. I have learned they are quite proud of *pintxos* here in the north, and if you call them tapas, expect a scolding.

We sip a glass of wine and order several rounds of these delicious morsels as rain falls outside of the open door next to our table. The fresh musty smell of warm summer rain adds a welcome perfume to our dining experience.

"So I guess we need to recalculate," I tell Amy as she is scarfing down a particularly delicious bite of fish.

"I guess we do," she replies. "We didn't make it very far yesterday, and we definitely didn't plan for bed bugs!"

We open the guidebook to crunch some numbers to see if it still might be possible for us to finish in the days we have left. We have

18 days to go, and after some investigation, it's still possible. Yet with every setback, more challenging. Before heading back to the hotel, we spot a *farmacia* that is actually open despite the holiday.

"Tengo chinches," I tell the woman behind the counter inside. *I have bed bugs.* She smiles as I am sure I have said something that doesn't translate very well. "Que tienes?" *What do you have?* I ask her, hoping for a solution.

Without wasting any time, she pulls a small box off the shelf and hands it to me. She explains that it is a powerful bug repellent especially good at keeping the bed bugs from eating you. She recommends I spray it in my pack and on each bed I sleep on along the Way. I thank her for the advice, and we head out the door with my new chemical weapon in hand.

The bed back in our hotel is incredibly comfortable. It is like lying on a cloud, and the silence of no snoring roommates quickly sends me into a deep sleep. Hopefully my hard work has paid off, and I will not wake up tomorrow with new bites. Tomorrow we enter the famous *Meseta*.

Arrival Day: St. Jean Pied-de-Port

Day 1: Trail Marker Pyrenees Mountains

Day 4: Descent From Clouds

Day 9: Sleeping Mats at Church of St. John the Baptist
Grañon

PART TWO

THE MESETA

Just try not to take
life so seriously, peregrino.

Fernanda, Pilgrim from Spain
Trail Day 13

You will not make it
to Santiago de Compostela.

Bar Owner
Trail Day 15

The Meseta

I wake up in the morning and immediately walk into our swanky bathroom, strip down, and check myself for new bed bug bites. I am relieved to find nothing. No new bites last night, so I think I may have shaken them. The real test will be when I have to sleep in my sleeping bag again at the next albergue. Surely my bag is where they have taken up residence. I liberally spray my new bug killer in my pack just to be sure.

We head out the door at 5 a.m. to find the streets of Burgos still filled with drunken people from the local festival last night. Some young drunk Spaniards yell at us from their second story window, "Buuuennnn Caminnnno, pererrrrregrinos!" A few others try to start a deep conversation with us about our purpose for walking. They are too drunk, and it is too early, so I pretend I don't speak Spanish, and we make our way through the cobblestone streets.

We pass the giant cathedral again on our way out of the city center. It is beautiful at this hour. Like an old wise man, the cathedral seems to watch us as we walk, peering down at the two Americans making their way towards Santiago. We are alone now. There are no drunken partiers in sight. The Moon hangs in the sky just above the tall cathedral towers and looks as if it was placed there by a skilled artist's hand. Moonbeams highlight the stone gargoyles above our heads.

We head out of town, eventually stopping for some tortilla española and some café con leche. Energized by breakfast and back on the trail, we finally enter the famous *Meseta*! Up to this point, many a conversation turns to the *Meseta*. Whether it be dreaded or sublime, all have their opinions and anticipation for what many consider to be the "mental" section of the Camino de Santiago. We are finishing the first leg, which is considered the "physical" section because it tests your body with more difficult terrain. I can definitely attest to the physical part and am ready for something less strenuous.

The *Meseta*, which in Spanish translates to the plateau, is a long section of land in the middle of Spain that is flat and covered with fields of wheat, barley, and oats.[1] Poppies dot the landscape, but other than that, there is very little shade, and the heat becomes intense. It is considered the mental section of the trek because there is no longer much to look at. It becomes you alone with brown fields, the sun, and your thoughts. A place that can drive you mad. I look forward to the challenge. We trudge on, officially entering the *Meseta* and finding the land to be completely flat as advertised.

It reminds me of Kansas, but it's also surprisingly scenic. You can see for miles around, and to find yourself standing in the middle of a foreign country with a huge blue sky overhead, in complete solitude, is the stuff of adventure. It energizes me.

I am thankful for the less hilly terrain, which will provide my knees with a much needed break. The constant ups and downs of our first 12 days have really tested my tendons. Sweat drips down my head as each hour passes, and one wheat field blends into the next. As usual I am in a lot of pain today and almost everywhere hurts. The heat intensifies the swelling, which does not help. During a break, I grab our Camino journal and jot down a list of ailments that I am currently experiencing. "Check out this list! This is ridiculous!" I laugh, showing my injury list to Amy. She finds it even more hilarious than I do and can't seem to stop laughing.

- right Achilles hurts
- both knees swollen
- right shoulder very tender (from leaning on Dolores)
- left hamstring on fire
- blister on right hand (from Dolores)
- bed bug bites on back, shoulders and hand
- right toe tendon starting to hurt

In contrast, Amy seems to be improving. "I feel good today!" She explains. "I don't even think I will need a nap. My body is getting used to 30-kilometer days!"

"Must be the yoga," I snap back.

As we walk through the intense heat, we meet a girl named Fernanda from Spain. She looks to be in her late 20s and wears a big smile set below kind dark eyes. She is wearing a big straw hat similar to ours, which breaks the ice. We speak in Spanish about our hats, the heat, and—as seems to be common out here—we quickly skip the small talk, and I ask why she is walking the Camino de Santiago.

"No tengo trabajo," she explains. *I don't have a job.* I feel a pang of jealousy. What freedom she must have! This thought instantly makes me feel crazy.

She is walking because it's cheap, and frankly, why not? It is almost a right of passage for Spaniards, and now is the perfect time. The economy in Spain is still struggling, especially for the younger demographic. Almost half of Spanish youth are unemployed, and Fernanda is one of them.[2] I naively explain that I have not found my passion yet and that is part of the reason I am out here. She breaks out into laughter, which confuses me. I ask her what is so funny.

"Que Americano," she laughs. *How American.*

This catches me off guard, and I ask her what she means. Finding your passion for work, she explains, is such an American way of thinking. She tells me that she would be happy to get any job as long as it is secure and stable. The concept of loving your job is not something most of her friends strive for. We work to live. We don't live to work. Sure, it is great if you like your job, but she cannot understand my angst wanting to find my passion. Her identity is not derived from what she does to make money.

Fernanda reminds me that so many countries, even worse off than Spain, have people who would love my banker's hours of 8 a.m. to 5 p.m., retirement benefits, and my air-conditioned office. They might even appreciate the cubes, which I loathe with a burning intensity. Finding your passion is a luxury reserved for those who are lucky enough to live in a country that has a multitude of options. She sees the embarrassment on my sweaty face as her words sink in, and she begins to use a kinder tone.

"But it's OK," Fernanda says. She kicks a small stone off the dry dirt trail. "We all come from different places and have different paths. Just try not to take life so seriously, peregrino!"

There are probably hundreds, if not thousands, of people walking the Camino de Santiago at this very moment, and somehow I continue to meet the ones who hold the very lessons I need to learn.[3] An international perspective, I am reminded, can help you see yourself and your worldview in a whole new way. I need to start cultivating gratitude and focus on what I do have instead of what I don't.

We continue on the trail as the sun blazes down. I embrace the *Meseta* and try to think my way to some answers. *What do I have? What can I be grateful for?* My mind takes me back to downtown Denver. It is 2007. Amy and I have just moved in together. A big step in any relationship. I am two months into my "soul crushing" job at CBS. It has been a full year since my stint on the Travel Channel has ended, and I have been desperately trying to land another hosting gig. On a normal Tuesday, as I sit in my cube at work, miserable, my phone rings. It is the offer I have been waiting for. A small production company has been given the green light to produce a new travel show. They need a host, and I am offered the position. I would be traveling the world, seeking out the best summer music festivals, and my experiences would be put into season one of this yet to be named show. The vision is an Anthony Bourdain style approach but for music, not food. I am ecstatic. The only catch is that I would leave to begin filming in three weeks. Our first location would be Edinburgh, Scotland. I rush home to tell Amy the good news.

"Wait, what?" she replies to my explanation. "How long will you be gone?"

"Four months to start. But if the show goes well, and we get to film a second season, who knows." I explain.

"So you are just going to leave?" she says. She looks angry. Without saying another word she walks out of the apartment. After an hour, she returns with her thoughts composed. I can see she has been crying.

"I don't know if I can have a relationship with someone who is never home. If you are successful with this career path, you will never be here. Is that really what you want?" she explains.

"I don't know what I want, dammit!" I am frustrated because I know she is right. "All I know is I can't do what I am doing now for a second longer! Do you know what it is like to hate every second of the day while you are working?"

"When you make decisions out of emotion, the results will lead you to more frustration," she whispers in response to my raised voice.

I already know what I am going to do. Above all things, relationships are more important to me than any job. Deep down, I don't want a transient life full of long distance relationships. In the end, I make the excruciating decision to turn down the job and have now been happily married for five years. The one part of my life where I feel truly successful. Of course my mind still tells me that even though I made the choice, TV and radio is failure number two.

Resting in the sun on the side of the trail, I spot a man slowly approaching us. He looks like a wavy mirage through the heat rising from the ground. But as he gets closer I recognize him immediately. It is the Italian Thong Man! I elbow Amy, and we observe him as he approaches. He is still angry. Yelling to himself as he walks. A flood of curse words in multiple languages pours out of him, scattering on the trail in his wake. We wave buen Camino, but he barely looks up as he huffs and puffs down the trail. I wonder what he is mad about today and why he is here. I also wonder if that is what I have looked like today while lost in thought, limping through the brown fields. Ten hours of walking. Ten hours worth of thoughts as numerous as the stones on the trail.

Roman Way

"I need a day off," I tell Amy. My body simply does not want to walk. We both are dragging, and the morning's trek proves to be very slow going. Our 30-day timeframe leaves us no time to rest. A big mistake in the planning process, which I am now regretting. Despite the pain, it is a beautiful morning in the *Meseta*.

"I know, me too. Just take it slow today. We can take lots of breaks." Amy replies. We pass through old ruins along the trail as the amber golden light makes it's way through the morning air hitting the crumbling stones, illuminating them as if just for us.

I am focused on each slow step, willing my legs to carry me forward. Amy seems to be moving more slowly than normal, too, as we continue on, mostly in silence. There are not many people on the trail today, which I love. We are walking in the footsteps of Romans. Literally following a 2,000-year-old Roman road which used to carry common folk, politicians, and legions of Roman armies.[1] I imagine horses pulling chariots speeding by. Historical records show that the average horse drawn cart and chariot could travel 40 to 50 kilometers per day (25 to 31 miles) using these ancient highways.[2] We have been averaging 25 to 30 kilometers per day on foot. The trail is unusually straight today, which is a mark of Roman technology that allowed for such precise construction. Many of the roads are even built in such a way as to resist rain and flooding.[3] The trail is in great condition today.

We continue on for hours, stopping first for breakfast then lunch. The day seems to crawl by as the physical exhaustion is making it impossible to speed through the ancient terrain.

"It is nice to slow down and take it all in, don't ya think?" Amy asks. "So far, I think the Meseta is beautiful and kind of peaceful."

"I agree," I reply. "Not sure what all the fuss was about."

Conversation seems almost wrong in the solitude, so we both become lost in the rhythm of walking. Out here, silence truly is golden. By late afternoon, we have finally made it to Boadilla del Camino. A depressing sleepy village, population 140, with nothing more than a church, dusty streets, and a couple of albergues.[4] We stop at a fountain under the shade of a large grove of trees as we enter town.

A man surprises us, seeming to appear from nowhere, and strikes up a conversation. I can tell he is not a pilgrim.

"Where are you from?" he asks.

"United States," I reply. I can't place his accent, but his English is very good.

"Here, let me get you a drink of water," he says while reaching for our water bottles. "This is a Roman fountain you know."

At this point I feel uncomfortable. You can tell when someone's intentions are not conversation. I just haven't yet figured out what this guy is selling, but my instincts have put me on the defensive.

"Really? A Roman fountain?" Amy replies while handing him her water bottle. "How do you know?"

He fills Amy's bottle then mine and hands them back to us encouraging a sip, "Drink, drink!"

I take a long swig of the cool refreshing liquid. "It's good! Thanks," I nod.

"This is the best water on the Camino de Santiago!" he proclaims. "The Romans built their fountains in a way that keeps the water cool. The water is always cold no matter the temperature outside."

"It does taste like it came out of a fridge," I agree, nodding a bit too enthusiastically.

"You are drinking from a fountain that has been here for many years. The water of kings!" he continues on.

"Are you looking for somewhere to stay tonight?" he casually asks. There it is. He is a hospitalero. I glance over his shoulder, and behind him I see an albergue. The courtyard is completely empty and unnaturally void of any signs of life.

"No," I lie. My gut is telling me not to stay at his establishment. "We are going to walk to the next town today." His smile fades, and without saying another word, he pounces on a pair of unsuspecting pilgrims who have just entered town.

"Peregrinos, welcome! Did you know this is a Roman fountain?" he repeats the script. "Come, sit, drink!" We get up and unceremoniously leave.

"Do you think that was really a Roman fountain?" I ask Amy as we begin our search for somewhere else to stay.

"The guidebook did say there are Roman fountains scattered throughout this part of the Camino, so it could be," she speculates. "But who knows!"

We randomly select an albergue called *En El Camino* and enter the front gate to find an incredible oasis inside! A beautifully manicured dark green lawn, incredible Camino artwork, and a swimming pool for our aching bodies.

We take off our shoes, grab a bed for only 7 euro per person, and after the daily laundry and shower, head to the pool to soak our feet. The ice-cold water feels amazing on my aching lower half. We enjoy a well-deserved lazy afternoon sipping light Spanish beer poolside in the summer sun. A familiar face sits down next to us and pops his feet into the swimming pool. It is the man we saw the first day crossing the Pyrenees who was walking barefoot!

We strike up a conversation, and it turns out that he is from Bulgaria. To me, he is the spitting image of "the most interesting man in the world" from the beer commercials. He has slicked back gray hair and a well-kept beard. His feet seem to be in good shape, and he is a, for lack of a better word, buff man.

He is now retired, and it has been his dream to walk the Camino de Santiago for 30 years. He is also walking with his wife who is napping inside. Explaining that we saw him on the first day, I can't help but ask him about his feet.

"Ahhh yes they are good!" he laughs. His English level is very basic, so he struggles to explain. "I wear ummm. How do you say?" He points to his feet.

"Shoes," Amy helps him out.

"Yes shoes! I wear shoes when I walk on the black road. The. How do you say? Road. Pave road," he explains. "The black road is too hot! It burns my feet!"

Slowly, he continues on. I empathize with his frustration, trying to find the right words. Speaking another language can be maddening.

"I want to really experience and feel the earth beneath my feet," he taps the ground for effect. "I want to be a real pilgrim!"

I understand what he is trying to say. We have already seen many works of art depicting ancient pilgrims, and it seems that back in the day, pilgrims walked in sandals, sometimes barefoot, and carried only a small satchel and a gourd for water. All the while trusting that what they needed would be provided. The simplicity of the ancient Way. That is what this modern day pilgrim is looking for.

The lazy afternoon fades to night, and after a dinner of well-cooked lentil stew, we head off to bed. The albergue is absolutely packed. Amy and I are on separate top bunks in a room full of 20 or 30 people packed in like sardines. My thoughts turn to the infestation I may or may not still be carrying in my sleeping bag.

As I spray my bug repellent directly on the mattress, I am hoping that the bed bugs literally don't bite. It has been a few days since my episode in Burgos, and if they don't get me tonight, it will prove that I have successfully killed them. I stare at the ceiling, shut my eyes, and after what seems like a few minutes, open them again to find that it is morning. The sun has not yet risen, but the room is already bustling with life. Beams of light from headlamps flash around the room as pilgrims ready themselves for the day. Time to start walking again.

"No new bed bug bites," I sleepily tell Amy as we make our way out of Boadilla del Camino.

"Yaaawwwwwyyyyy!" she replies while letting out a long yawn.

Our oasis behind us, we enter the *Meseta* and start to eat up some kilometers before breakfast. We find ourselves immersed in a thick fog, which adds to the feeling of isolation. It is cold at this hour, and it is hard to see any progress as our visibility is quite limited.

Each morning brings a new sunrise, 15 Camino sunrises so far. Each with a personality of its own. Some bright, almost happy, and some somber, almost wise. Today's sunrise is eerily beautiful. We pass by a field of sunflowers not quite ready to bloom. Their giant stalks topped by their huge lifelike heads all facing the ground in unison as if praying to an invisible sun God. I can almost see them smile with relief when the first pink-yellow light of the day reaches their leaves through the morning fog.

I don't know why, but my body is feeling good for the first time since day one in France. We start to follow a wide canal at a healthy pace, and before long, our stomachs begin to growl for breakfast. The search is on for the first bar. We walk into the first place we see, and the owner takes one look at me as I limp inside to order and tells me that I am not going to make it.

"You have knee pain?" he aggressively asks. "Where?"

I point to just below my kneecap.

"You will not make it to Santiago de Compostela." He shakes his head. His co-worker emphatically nods in agreement.

"We see many pilgrims with knee pain. You will not make it," he repeats.

They both have managed to piss me off instantly, and I give him the best look of disapproval I can muster. Who does he think he is telling me I won't make it! "Yeah, well screw you," I whisper under my breath. Just quiet enough so they won't hear me. I storm out with my fresh squeezed orange juice and tortilla española.

"Mmmmmm that looks good," Amy digs in.

"Well the guy who made it is a prick," I reply.

"Huh?" Amy asks between bites.

"Nothing," I reply. "He told me I won't make it to Santiago."

"Wow. What a jerk. Better burn the place down," Amy sarcastically replies. "You can't run fast enough, though, so we better negotiate a getaway car first."

As we sip our coffee outside, we see our familiar international friends stop or pass and say good morning and buen Camino. The two Australians, Peter from Ireland, and an artist friend from London pass by and wave. After refueling, we continue on our way. I am in the zone today and physically improving. A wave of hope washes over me.

"I am feeling better!" I tell Amy. "It is amazing what changes 24 hours can bring."

"Me too!" she replies enthusiastically. We may be able to do this in 30 days! The walk today is not particularly beautiful as we follow highways carrying speedy cars but who cares! We are making great time.

The entire route today is completely flat, which is also giving my knees a much-needed break. We take our time passing through sleepy villages, stopping to take pictures of donkeys freely roaming the streets. As we eat a packed lunch of cheese and nuts while sitting on an old wooden bench, a pair of donkeys casually make their way to our location. They stop and stare at us like dogs begging for some food.

The brown landscape matches the brown walls of the villages out here as if camouflaged from an unseen enemy. We finally make our way to Carrión de los Condes. As we enter town, we are aggressively pursued on the street by people offering places to stay. We talk with one girl offering a private room at a hotel in town, and we agree on a price. She leads us through winding streets to the establishment, up some stairs, and sits us in front of the friendly hospitalero. We have been successfully fished from the street, but I don't care. A private room and sleep sounds great to me.

Again, I feel a twinge of guilt at opting for so many private rooms, but the experience of not sleeping and cramming into rooms full of people has not been something I have enjoyed up to this point. Still, I can't seem to shake the feeling that we should be in an albergue. That I am cheating somehow. We enjoy some dinner and rest before heading back to the room for sleep.

There is a skylight in our room, and I stare at a group of swallows flying in the sky above. The wind is strong, and the birds are struggling to stay in the air. I glance out the window to see giant storm clouds headed our way. Thunder rumbles in the distance. Tomorrow may be our first taste of bad weather. Hopefully we can keep our momentum despite what looks like definite rain.

As we try to sleep, I keep getting awakened by the neighboring room. There is a soccer game on, so the people in the room next to us (not pilgrims) are having a sort of party and have left the door open, TV cranked and booming. I can't take it anymore. I bolt out of bed at about 11 p.m. and storm directly into their room. If I were a cartoon character, there would have been steam coming out of my ears. They all freeze and stare at this half-dressed man who just limped into their room. I forgot to put my shirt on, and I still have a few leftover red bed bug bites all over my chest.

As I try to cuss them out in Spanish, I quickly realize I can't speak Spanish when I am angry, so I just stare at them, making awkward angry eye contact with the lot. Blood boiling and with as much fire as possible I finally yell something in English: "SHUT UP!"... *Well said, idiot. Now, leave.* I think to myself. I then storm out like some crazed madman. To my delight, my mini tantrum worked.

"You sure told them," Amy sleepily tells me before she starts to dream.

Achilles Tendinitis

Dark clouds and steady rain greet us as we again find ourselves walking on old Roman roads at five o'clock in the morning. Our usual method of drying our clothes by pinning them to our backpacks is not working out.

Today I am really trying to focus on living in the moment. It is easy on the Camino to think of the kilometers. Just like life, you become obsessed with where you are going and where you have been. You really have to remind yourself to enjoy the experience while it lasts.

The rain continues to drizzle down, but our light rain jackets keep us relatively dry. I am focusing on a quote I like from Eckhart Tolle and *The Power of Now*: "As soon as you honor the present moment, all unhappiness and struggle dissolve, and life begins to flow with joy and ease. When you act out the present-moment awareness, whatever you do becomes imbued with a sense of quality, care and love—even the most simple action." The simple action for today is walking, step-by-step, towards Santiago.

"It's really beautiful out here today," Amy observes.

"I know. What do you think it is about a pilgrimage that makes you grow as a person?" I ask.

She replies, "Maybe the fact that we are silent for hours. We're in nature with no distractions and getting a chance to hear our own true inner voice. No television, no iPhone, no internet. Nothing at all to distract you from the lessons you need to learn." We pass a clump of trees that break up the monotone gray mist; the tops of their branches are hidden in the fog.

"I agree," I tell Amy. "It seems like life has far too many distractions. Back home, any chance at a silent or calming moment is gone when we reach for our phones to see what's happening on Facebook, check out Instagram or whatever. At least I know I do. After which I always feel like crap because Facebook makes it seem like everyone else is having a way more fabulous life than I am. It is nice to have a break. I particularly love the fact that not a soul on Earth can call me right now. The phone will not ring. That is so liberating." We continue over a wet gravel trail for hours. The silence is a sort of walking meditation.

During a break, we meet a mother and daughter from Florida who are walking together, and we strike up an interesting conversation. Janice, the mother, just got done working as a doctor in Haiti and now works as an acupuncturist. She explains her craft, which sounds like a fascinating profession.

"Maybe I should become an acupuncturist," I tell Amy after they have moved ahead of us on the trail.

"Are you crazy!?" She laughs. "You hate needles!"

I tend to do this a lot. I latch on to any career idea that sounds interesting. This is a telltale sign of someone who is not satisfied with his or her own work life. I have toyed with the idea of becoming a school psychologist because, well, Amy is one, and she seems to like it. After job shadowing her, I realized that kids are terrifying little beasts. Cute, but it's not a career for me. I once obsessed over the possibility of becoming a doctor. The only problem being I hate blood. I also have a new business idea weekly. Recently, after watching a movie, I decided I should make furniture from the beetle kill wood in Colorado. The only problem is I have never made a piece of furniture in my life. "Yeah, you have a point," I agree with Amy. "Just a thought."

Many of my career aspirations have been based on what I think is a well respected and even prestigious career. As I get a little bit older, I am starting to seriously doubt if I can get my purpose from work. Maybe the Spanish girl we met a few days ago, Fernanda, had a point. Maybe work is the wrong place to look for meaning. I have started to value freedom over prestige. I want to make my own hours. I want more Camino de Santiago's in my life and less time spent commuting to work.

We trudge on through the light but constant drizzle of rain. The walking motion is therapeutic and calming today. Many pilgrims are wearing large rain ponchos that cover themselves and their backpacks. They look like giant upright sea turtles, wrapped in trash bags, slowly moving forward. After a few hours, we stop for a quick snack of dried fruit and meet a giant man from Norway.

He looks like a warrior towering above us with an equally impressive voice. He tells us that he has done the Camino once before. That first attempt ended when he slipped on some mud and fell, severely injuring his back. He has returned this year to try it again. He is not looking too good, though. As he separates from us, I notice that he is limping on both legs, which have two giant knee braces wrapped around them for support. He has two walking sticks, and his pack looks like it weighs more than I do.

A few more hours pass in gray silence.

During another break, we meet two bicycle pilgrims. A father and son from Australia, conquering the Camino de Santiago on two wheels. I find them hilarious. At 11 a.m., dad is puffing cigarettes as they discuss grabbing some breakfast beers! Athletes certainly come in all forms out here. Amy and I sit on a log outside of the sleepy bar they just entered and are invited inside.

"Want a beer?" the son asks.

"I'm good! Bit early for me," I reply.

"Nonsense!" Dad replies. A huge cloud of cigarette smoke billowing from his mouth. "It is good for the blood and even better for your mind!"

We leave the pair to their beer and get back to the trail. We meet a divorced solar panel installer from San Francisco whose brother has left him behind on the Way. The Camino de Santiago magic helps us quickly skip small talk and get to the heart of his reason for walking.

"Why are you here?" I ask.

"Divorce is hard," he replies. "Really hard. I needed to get away and think."

"And your brother?" I ask. "Why did you two separate? You came here to walk together right?"

An exasperated grin spreads across his face and he replies, "Well. I guess he needed to get away from me and think."

By midafternoon, the sun still has yet to appear. It looks like I will be wearing the same clothes tomorrow. If anything, the clean clothes strapped to our packs are wetter than when we started out this morning. We make our way into another sleepy village, Terradillos de Templarios, population 78.[1] We get lucky and score two beds in the albergue in a room with only five beds total. Our chances of sleep are good! We enter the room and are surprised to find Peter from Ireland! He is one of our roommates for the night.

After a nap, another amazing communal dinner awaits us in the main area of the albergue. We dine with our friend Peter, the two walking Australians Aaron and Blake, and the artist from London. This will be our fourth dinner with these same people, and the night is an awesome international affair. The World Cup is on. Italy is playing, and some Italian flags apparently stuffed in Camino backpacks make an appearance as their owners scream for their team. Our Brazilian friends are even staying here as everyone is crammed into this small space, sharing stories, food and dark red Spanish wine. We split our time between watching the World Cup and getting to know everyone at our table better.

Aaron and Blake are walking the Camino for the adventure of it. Nothing more. They have been friends for almost 20 years, and they try to take on some kind of adventure every year together. Both are athletes through and through. Each is easily over 6 feet, 5 inches with rough beards and muscular builds. They used to play rugby together, and I can tell that they could easily break me in half if they tried. Now in their early 40s, they remain in fantastic shape.

"What was your name again?" I say turning to the artist from London. "I am sorry I am terrible with names."

"Sam," She says smiling. She has curly blond hair, blue eyes, and looks to be in her late 30s.

"So what is your story? Why are you here, Sam?" Amy asks.

"I actually came here with my mum," she replies in a thick British accent. "I was only supposed to be here for a week, for vacation, but I couldn't go home. I just couldn't. I have to keep walking. The Camino pulls you in like that I guess. My mum went home, and I just stayed."

"What kind of art do you make?" Blake asks.

"I work with glass. So I make things like bowls and bigger art pieces for collectors," she explains. "I have actually managed to lose a client because of this. The Camino. They wanted me to get back to finish a project I have been working on, and I just can't."

She looks sad so I decide to pry. "Is there any other reason you don't want to go back?"

"I actually just got divorced. Not a nice guy really. I was married for four years, and well, now it's time to move on. I think I might keep traveling after this. Maybe a year or so, I don't know. I need to refresh my spirits. Eat some good food. Find God, whoever she might be," she smiles.

"Like the book! *Eat, Pray, Love*," I joke. Sam rolls her eyes and simultaneously Amy punches me in the shoulder. "What did I say!?" I protest.

"I guess you could say that," Sam replies, amused.

"I am no longer a wife, I don't have kids, I don't know that I will ever have kids, or meet someone new," she pauses for a while. We all take a sip of wine and poke at our plates. "It is just a lot of unknowns you know. It is scary. The only thing I do know is that I can't sit in my depressing apartment in London with my cats to figure this out."

"Well I think you are the bravest person I have met so far on the trail," Blake says.

Sam blushes. "Thank you. That is a really nice thing to say."

After hours of wonderful conversation, we finally make our way to our room to get some sleep. Amy sums up our night as she scribbles a quick note in our Camino journal: *"Favorite Memory: Spending time over dinner and drinks chatting with new friends. We went to bed late! 10:30!"*

I drift off to sleep quickly. That is until a thunderous snore wakes us at 4 a.m. I scan the room. This trucker type of snore is coming from a woman lying in the bed right next to us. It seems to vibrate my bed with an incredible strength like a clap of thunder. I glance at Amy. She is awake too and looks at me in a sleepy haze. I look around the room, annoyed. Everyone is awake except the snorer. I whisper to Amy, "I won't be able to sleep through this."

"I can't either," she sleepily replies.

We both know what the other is thinking. We strap on our headlamps, brush our teeth and head out the door. It is time to start walking. It is 4:30 in the morning.

"How is it possible for the human body to create that noise?!" Amy is angry.

We stumble out the front gate of the albergue, half sleepwalking in a sort of delirious state. I can't stop laughing. It is a crazy person's laugh. One born out of exhaustion. On one hand, it is hilarious that this lady, who inspired our early departure, could snore with such skill. On the other hand, sleep deprivation is becoming a problem, and we are a bit grumpy to say the least.

It is pitch dark at this hour, and we walk by the light of our headlamps. A sea of stars twinkle above us as we slowly leave the village and make our way forward. There are no streetlights and no cities glowing in the distance. Just a beautiful uninterrupted natural darkness.

Our only companions are dozens of snails spread out on the trail. They must be morning animals because they are everywhere. They are hard to see outside of the beam of the headlamps and every once in a while our shoes fall on a poor unsuspecting creature. CRUNCH!

Light slowly creeps into the day. Black fades to gray, which fades to a soft pink and a golden sunrise. We can finally see our terrain, and like most of the *Meseta,* it is nothing spectacular. Just flat fields upon flat fields interrupted by small pueblos sprinkled here and there. I listen to music to keep me going.

As we continue to walk, I notice something alarming. My Achilles' heel is beginning to ache. Not just typical soreness but I am worried something is very wrong. The hours pass. We see familiar faces as we make our way through the day, and my worry continues to grow. I don't dare look at it. Not yet.

By late afternoon, we make it to the final stretch of the day. A long vast open sky hovers overhead as I tenderly make my way over a deserted dirt path. We have not seen anyone for hours, and we stop several times to double and triple check our guidebook, making sure that we are not lost. We have not seen a town for hours, and it seems like we should have made it to one by now.

I know something is very wrong with my body, but I push on in silence. No need to worry Amy quite yet, so I keep it to myself. Our two Australian friends finally pass us, confirming that we are not lost. They are the only humans we see for the next two hours until we finally make our way to the tiny town of Calzadilla de los Hermanillos.

We check in to a very nice albergue and sit outside to rest on the patio. Mustering up some courage, I take off my right sock to survey the damage. A wave of emotion passes over me as I see an incredibly swollen and red Achilles' heel. I log on to the internet, and over the next hour, the hope of the previous days fades slowly away with each bit of information I gather.

I have the exact symptoms of Achilles tendinitis, and everyone's advice is to stop immediately. What's more, I have been walking with Achilles tendinitis for the last five days or so. A characteristic sign is pain in the morning, which gradually subsides, fooling you into thinking it is getting better.[2] Apparently this is a common injury on the Camino de Santiago. It can eventually lead to a sudden rupture when you will hear a loud snap as your Achilles tendon suddenly separates and curls up into your calf. You will then be in the worst pain of your life and need surgery.[3] I realize this is the end, for now. We need to stop and rest and decide what to do from there. This new reality slowly sinks in despite my denial.

I am incredibly angry and sad, and my bruised ego almost leads me to tears. I feel my old friend creep into my mind. Failure. A new kind of failure. My body has never prevented me from completing something. Word quickly spreads among friends as our Australian friend pops his head around the corner, and I see disappointment on his face.

"I heard the news, Gabe," he says in a thick accent. "It's really that bad?" he innocently asks. I guess another lesson I am supposed to learn. Plans are futile on the Camino and in life. I know his look, though. He thinks I am being weak. Maybe I am.

We sit down to dinner, and I am steaming. It feels like another failure to add to my list. My thoughts of being average are only emphasized by this new event. My head tells me, "You can't even *walk* across a country." The food comes, and not even a particularly flavorful gazpacho can lighten my mood.

I am sitting with Janice, the doctor now acupuncturist from Texas, and her daughter whom we met a few days ago. They are doing their best to cheer me up. They remind me of the Camino shell, "Everyone has their own path to Santiago. We have already taken one bus! It's no big deal!" I am trying to stay positive and learn from this.

"You know you are the one putting all this pressure on yourself," Amy chimes in. "No one else on planet Earth really cares if you take a few days to rest and then continue on. If you take a break and cover some of the trail by train it doesn't mean you have not finished the Camino de Santiago."

Our new plan is to take a train tomorrow to León and rest for one full day after that, in hopes that we can then finish the rest of the Camino on foot. Thankfully, Amy's usual positive outlook on things is helping a little. I am so glad to have her on this journey with me.

Defeated and depressed, I head upstairs with a bag of ice to rest. Our outlook is shaky at best. My mind won't turn off tonight.

Is this this end? Did we fly all the way to Spain to fail? Have we failed? What is wrong with me? Why am I so average?

"What ya thinkin about?" Amy asks as she places the bag of ice on the back of my heel. It is tender, and it is hard to imagine walking again anytime soon.

"Oh you know. Stuff," I reply.

"You are not a failure. Here or in life. You will be, though, if you continue to measure your life by comparing yourself to others," she says while correctly reading my mind. I know she is right, but I can't shake the feeling.

Rest

"Dos zumos de naranja," the friendly hospitalera says. *Two orange juices*. She sets down two fresh squeezed orange juices in front of us. It is 9 a.m. We woke up late, and our plan for the day is to get to León by any method that does not include walking. I look around to find nobody. All of the pilgrims have already left for the day. A ping of jealousy hits me. I wish I were already walking, too. I desperately want to finish this trek to simply prove to myself that I can actually see something through. It is a win that I need at this point in my life. The hospitalera is very helpful as we start to plan our escape.

We run into the type of difficulties you might expect when stranded in the middle of nowhere in Spain. There is a bus. But it runs every other day. Not today though. Damn. There is a taxi! But there is only one, and he is busy. There is a train! But this requires the taxi to drive us to the station, which is in the next town over. Deep breaths. We end up lining up the taxi for later in the afternoon and spend the next few hours just sitting with our thoughts and wallowing in my disappointment.

I take the time to examine the contents of my pack. Without water, my pack weighs 7 kilos, or just over 15 pounds. This is much lighter than most of the pilgrim's packs along the Way. For example, The Barista told me his pack weighed close to 20 kilos! Before we started this journey, many warned us to take only the bare minimum. The general rule is to make sure you carry no more than 10% of your body weight. Advice that I have heeded, but I want to make sure, trying to find an answer, something I can blame for my injury.

I lay everything out on the bed upstairs piece by piece, starting with my clothes. There are two t-shirts, one long sleeve shirt, a lightweight black rain jacket, shower sandals, the bottoms of my convertible zip off pants, and two pairs of gray specialty hiking wool socks. I only brought two extra pairs of underwear, which I lay next to my extra pair of gym shorts. The gym shorts I wear in the evenings while my other clothes are drying on the line. I search for something I can throw away to lighten my load, which is a pointless exercise but helps my mind focus on something else.

Next I find the electrical converter, which is a bulky black beast. I was too cheap to buy a new, lighter weight converter before the trip, but this is essential to charging our camera and phones, so I can't throw it away. I keep digging. There is a lightweight sleeping bag, headlamp, sunscreen, blister kit, a Canon digital SLR camera and a dry sack to protect it from the rain. A small, blue quick-dry towel, my human shammy after showers on the trip, is placed next to my neck scarf. All that is left are earplugs, small travel toiletries, ibuprofen cream, a lightweight Moleskine notebook that is acting as our Camino journal, the guidebook, a rain cover for the pack and the things I will be wearing daily. Including my large brimmed straw hat to keep the sun at bay, knee brace, sunglasses, and my trail running shoes. Nothing is discardable to me, and I quickly repack, leaving room only for my self-pity. I am sure I will be carrying that for a while, too.

We stay until midafternoon when the next wave of pilgrims starts to arrive. We meet a couple from Colorado and a group of young guys who are from the U.S. but studying to become priests in Rome. These future priests are obviously walking the Camino during a school break for religious purposes, and they lighten my mood as they joke around with each other as only early 20-something guys can do. One of them is sick and has been throwing up along the trail all day.

His friends have just ordered food and are doing their best to make sure that the aromas reach their friend who is turning green. He looks terrible. "Mmmmmm fish stew," his friend jokes. Another friend makes fake gagging noises while laughing.

Amy offers him some charcoal pills. She has been carrying them just in case one of us gets sick but offers them to the young man. His name is Cole. He explains that they stayed in a monastery a couple of days ago, and the sisters who lived there made them a soup that has been causing stomach issues ever since, most likely a result of food poisoning. Amy explains that charcoal is extremely absorbent, and if he has food poisoning, the charcoal will absorb the bad stuff in his belly. At least in theory. He will most likely puke it all up again but the point is to get it all out of his system. Suspiciously, he obliges and says, "Bottoms up!" while downing the pill. His friends laugh with delight.

"Why are you guys out here?" I ask Cole.

"We are looking for God," he replies. "I want him to tell me how he can use me best in this world."

I guess I am not the only one looking for purpose out here.

The taxi finally comes for us, and I feel a wave of embarrassment. The moment is, in a word, ironic. I think about the teachers I judged for taking buses every other day. I think of the artist from California who invited us to share a taxi with her to the next town. I have judged all of them as my ego snugly put itself in a "better than you" category. I was supposed to be the "real" pilgrim. We step inside the taxi and are whisked away.

When we arrive in the next town, we have some more time to kill before the train arrives to take us to León. Amy and I sit down for a café con leche, and I am visibly enraged and shaken.

As usual Amy, my psychologist wife, is some sort of wise angel sent to talk the inner idiot out of me and bring me back to reality. She asks me some great questions, "Did we come here to walk the Camino for athletic reasons?"

I reply with my usual frown, "No. Not exactly."

She continues, "Is this some sort of race that states you must walk every step to truly be a pilgrim?"

"I guess not," I reply.

"Is every person's Camino the same?" her questions keep coming. "Are we in Spain and don't you *love* Spain?"

I take a moment to look around and try to remind myself of the situation. A busy waiter runs between tables taking orders as locals are doing what they do best in Spain, enjoying life. An outdoor European café in the warm June summer air. What could be better?

"What is so bad about resting and continuing at a slower pace?" she asks. "You need to get over it."

I start to calm down.

"Ok. You got me. You have a point," I say taking a deep breath.

In the middle of our conversation, a man walks up to our table off the street and drops a bag in front of us. I see inside big red ripe cherries. They are from his tree, and he makes us both take a handful. I try to give him some euro. "No no no! Eat! Strength for you to arrive to Santiago, peregrino," he protests. His treat.

My mood starts to improve. I glance at a quote in our guidebook, which is exactly what I need to hear: *"Here inside of me is a force that makes its own weather, winning through the thickest clouds to the shining sun." —John Brierley*

I decide to make my own weather and enjoy the adventure. Even if it is not the adventure I thought I was supposed to be having. We hobble over to the saddest train station in the world to catch our train, and it feels incredibly weird! The parking lot is cracked and filled with weeds. The station itself, yellow paint peeling from its walls, is locked. We are the only humans in sight. We are surrounded by fields and abandoned buildings. The buildings are half complete from Spain's construction boom days, no doubt foiled by the economic crash of 2008.[1] Someone's ambitions crumbling into a weathered heap of concrete and steel.

Apart from the taxi we just took, we have not been in anything motorized for 17 days, and it feels unnatural waiting for a train. We snap a quick picture to commemorate the occasion, and I grab my

Camino shell, rubbing my fingers over the grooves leading to the base. "There are many ways to Santiago," I repeat to myself. That is a mantra I can't forget.

The train finally comes, and 32 minutes later we arrive in León. Amy and I look at each other with amusement when we arrive. That would have taken us two days to walk! Hopefully the next few days bring some much-needed recovery to my injured body. This will determine the final leg of our journey, and I want to finish it on foot. There could be worse places to be stranded as well. León is supposed to be an amazing and beautiful city.

Recovery

Upon arriving by train, we spend the afternoon and evening in León simply staying off of our feet. Glorious. We have opted for a hotel since most albergues on the Camino de Santiago require you to leave after one night. We have discovered a new problem as well. Amy has a fresh set of brand new bed bug bites. As an easy solution, we chuck her sleeping bag in a dumpster before checking into the hotel. We have rarely needed it due to the heat this time of year in Spain, and it won't be missed. She repeats the heated washing process on her clothes, washing them with care in the sink and drying her clothes with a hair dryer in our room. She then sprays the inside of her bag with the powerful bug spray.

We sleep well. In the morning, we decide to hobble into the city center to see what this city is all about. My frustration from yesterday is turning into peace with our decision. I am trying to focus on the quote from our guidebook about making your own weather. I make a decision to let go of the disappointment and embrace the adventure. León proves to be a beautiful city.

This is my first time back since living in Spain, and dammit, I am going to enjoy every second no matter what my body is doing. We gingerly stroll through the cobblestone streets, past Roman remains, ancient city walls and bustling cafés as the signature Spanish legs of *jamón* hang above patrons' heads. We make our way to the cathedral in the city center. It's a spectacular structure, towering hundreds of feet above our heads almost sparkling in the midday sun. Pilgrims mix with locals and tourists alike as we all stare up at this giant work of art, mouths half open.

We choose a café and sit al fresco in front of the cathedral in the center of town. I am making an effort to eat what Google tells me is good for repairing injuries and order a fresh squeezed orange juice (Vitamin C is supposed to help repair your body), and we simply sit, enjoying one of the greatest spectator sports in the world, a busy *plaza mayor* in Spain. Like flies on a wall, we observe weary pilgrims entering the square sitting down and staring up. A pilgrim enters the square riding a horse and his panting dog follows. Tourists treat him almost as a celebrity asking for his picture, some lying down on the ground trying to get an artsy shot attempting to catch the cathedral in the background. A man selling giant balloons slowly circles the crowd every now and then, handing a bright balloon to an excited child. I overhear some American study abroad students who are sitting nearby, sketching the cathedral for an art class.

All of a sudden, we see Tom emerging from the crowd! This is the man we met many days ago in Grañon who is walking in memory of his recently deceased daughter. He pulls up a chair, and we share a relaxing hour together. I really like this man, and we talk about the journey so far, our injuries, and how everything is going. I can tell his deep-seated pain still hangs around him like a ghost, barely visible but there. After a while, it is time for him to move on, and we say our goodbyes. As it turns out, we will never see Tom again. "Buen Camino," I say with sincerity as he walks away. I love these random meetings with pilgrims. There's no pressure to make conversation, and we are free to live completely in the moment, just enjoying the company and then moving on.

Amy and I decide to make sure our tour of the city is very brief because I am supposed to be resting, and every step counts. Before we head back to the hotel, we feast on some delicious Spanish fare.

Lentil soup, salmon, and stuffed red peppers baked with Manchego cheese. Between courses, we savor big green olives, roasted almonds, and *Jamón Ibérico*. The dark red cured thin cut slices of meat holding the complex nutty flavor I have grown to adore. Iberian ham is about as free range as you can get and comes from the black hoof pigs that are allowed to roam in oak groves to feed on herbs, acorns, and grass. All of these combining into a cured meat that has a flavor all its own. Oh, how I love Spanish food!

Between bites, we map out the rest of our adventure. Tomorrow we will take a bus far enough to allow ourselves to finish the Camino by walking fewer kilometers per day. Instead of 25 to 30 kilometer days, we will plan for an average of 18 kilometers per day to finish as we walk through Galicia. This seems like a good plan as Galicia is supposed to be beautiful. Of the three sections of the Camino de Santiago, physical, mental, and spiritual, Galicia is the spiritual leg of this journey. It seems appropriate that we slow down for the last leg.

We will be missing out on essentially four recommended walking days or stages of the Camino de Santiago. We will be seeing those stages by bus. A total of 132.2 kilometers, or about 82 miles. I don't mind missing the outskirts of León, as we have heard they are very ugly, but a ping of regret and resentment again surfaces. I grab my Camino shell yet again as a bit of comfort, rubbing my fingers over the grooves. I am focusing on 82 miles out of 500, letting them make me bitter and angry. Isn't that how life is? Instead of cultivating gratitude for what we have accomplished, allowing it to grow within us, we focus on the few bad seeds in life. Allowing them to cast a shadow far greater than the actual problem.

My anger shifts its focus to life back home. Many pilgrims out here don't have a set day they must finish by. If they need to rest, they do it. They are simply walking, as carefree as the wind, taking as many days as they need to finish. I, on the other hand, have a flight to catch and only 30 days before I will be whisked away to a job I must get back for. It is hard to take a full month off work, and my vacation is unpaid. I feel like a caged creature who has been let out into the wild to roam, exploring with the pent up thirst for a more natural habitat. All the while realizing it is temporary, trying to squeeze every last drop out of my freedom, before the inevitable return to the cage. The cubicle.

After strategizing and our midday feast, we head to our room to sit and rest. We binge on television news, catching up on what has happened in the world over the past few weeks. After a good night's sleep I wake up feeling refreshed. I do a body scan to see how rest has affected my body. I am happy to see the swelling is going down in my heel, but mentally I am still terrified that any step could cause a snap of my Achilles. My knee swelling has gone down as well. We catch our bus and head to Villafranca del Bierzo. I stare out of the window at the pilgrims we speed past. Trying not to let myself think about what should have been. We are not the only pilgrims on this bus.

"How ya doin?" I ask Amy.

"I'm great!" she replies. "And side note. I think if St. James himself had the option to take an *ALSA* bus for part of this walk, he wouldn't have hesitated for a second. Especially if he had holy anointed Achilles tendinitis!"

After a few hours, we find ourselves in a green and lush countryside that I don't recognize as Spain. It looks more like Scotland. We find an albergue that the guidebook says has a reputation for bed bugs. But I don't want to walk anymore than I have to, so we check in anyway. We have already had a bout with these creatures, and I guess my fear is gone. The bites are not any more annoying than a mosquito bite, so we will live if they get us again.

As we settle into our new accommodations, I look around and do not recognize any of the pilgrims staying here. We have left our group far behind. I feel like the new kid in school as we keep to ourselves in the corner. The solitude doesn't last for long, though, as a group dinner with pilgrims brings yet another incredible night and opportunity to make new friends.

We sit at a large long wooden table in the large dining room, which fits in with this medieval looking town. The conversation is rich, and as we dine on local veggies, wine, and homemade olives from the hospitalero's olive trees, we learn about this albergue and its storied past. The hospitalero, an older Spanish man in his late 70s dressed in a bright yellow shirt and suspenders, tells us the story of his albergue. He is filled with pride at his life's work.

He and his brother built this place 18 years ago, stone by stone. Even some of the stones in the walls come from exotic international locations. "We wanted the soul of the Camino de Santiago reflected in the building," he passionately explains. "This albergue is a vehicle for peace. It took us four years to finish it. During construction, we asked our friends to bring us stones from all over Spain and from all over the world. They would usually bring one stone, so it took a long time! I have touched almost every stone in those walls, and everything you see I built with my hands. Do you see that one there?" He points to a small rounded rock in the wall near the floor.

Our eyes follow his extended finger.

"That one is from Portugal," he points to another. "That one up there in the corner. The white one. That one is from Germany."

All of our eyes are examining the walls, completely engrossed in the story. There are pictures on the stone walls from the man's youth, and dark wooden exposed beams cross the ceiling high over our heads. A dusty Brazilian flag hangs from under one of the windows. Next to that a plastic leg of Jamón hangs from a wooden pole embedded in the wall. On another window seal rests two golden plastic maneki-neko cats from Japan.

"The food is really good," I say, complimenting the chef. "How do you make the olives?"

"Well my trees make them," he laughs. "It is pretty simple. Just pick them, put them in salt water and leave them for a few months."

"Did you make this wine, too?" I ask.

"No, but it is from Galicia," he replies. Apparently it is too expensive to bottle so most wines from this region go directly from the cask to your cup. Including the wine we are having with dinner.

"We reuse these wine bottles. My neighbor makes the wine. I just buy it from him, and he fills up these wine bottles every few days for us," he explains. A foodie and a passionate soul. My kind of guy.

Day 13: Virgen del Manzano Church

Day 14: Albergue En El Camino

Day 15: Pilgrim Highway

Day 20: The Cathedral León

PART THREE

THE PENCIL

What would you do if
you knew you couldn't fail?

Tezka, Pilgrim from Slovenia
Trail Day 23

The Camino de Santiago sharpens you
into your greatest and truest form.

Hector, Hospitalero
Trail Day 27

The Meaning of Life

After another night of half sleeping to the tune of a room full of restless pilgrims, we get back on the trail. It feels good to be walking again and the few days of rest have really helped my body. Amy and I both are already loving this decision and now being able to walk less per day gives us more time to enjoy. If our walk were a movie, this would be where the corny inspirational music would pick up after the last few days of adversity. The walk today takes us through lush green valleys filled with roaring rivers. Mountains crammed with huge green trees surround us in every direction, almost encouraging our slow progress. I can already tell Galicia is going to be beautiful.

"Only nine days left," I say to Amy. I try to think of an appropriate mantra for the first day of the spiritual leg of the Camino de Santiago. I was hoping to be struck with, well, the meaning of life on this journey. So far it has not come to me. I ask Amy casually, "So let's figure this out, the meaning of life."

I must have been high on ibuprofen or something, but as we talk I think we might actually be on to something!

"Love," Amy says simply. "I think love is number one."

I push her a little asking, "How is that a meaning of life?"

"Think about all of the answers to all of life's problems," she explains as our walking sticks steadily clunk against the paved trail. "Think of the kindness of the man who rubbed your legs with olive oil in Grañon. And The Barista who gave you things from his pack to help you continue in Pamplona. Love and kindness. That is the path to happiness, and that is one of my meanings of life. If you truly want your life to matter, then maybe it is not on the huge grand scale you are striving for. Maybe you should spread kindness and love to individuals you meet. You will make small ripples in the grand scheme of things and your life will have mattered, even if only to a few."

The weight of Amy's words hits me in the face like a giant gust of wind. I pause, letting her words sink in. "Are you some sort of guru or something?" I say only half joking. "That actually makes a lot of sense."

We continue on, passing through a small village. I notice the buildings are built from dark gray stones in this part of Spain. A stark difference from the light tan rocks we have seen throughout this country so far, the result of a changing landscape and soil.

"I wish we didn't have to make money," I say. "Love doesn't pay the bills, does it?"

"Yeah, but that doesn't matter. Money has never motivated you or me," she replies.

"Maybe it should at least a little bit," I reply. "If we had more money, maybe we wouldn't have to work as much."

"You hate trust fund babies, and the rest of the rich work more than you would want to," she argues.

"I think I hate trust fund kids because I secretly want to be one," I reply.

"Do you really want to be *that guy* that works all the time, takes business trips, never sees his family or friends, lives for work, just so you can buy a nicer car, bigger house, pay for the sports package cable channels and buy ridiculous things to fill your ridiculous house?" She asks while pausing to look at me. "Money will not buy you purpose that is for sure."

"I know. I know," I reply. "I can't have it both ways. I just think money could buy freedom. I should start an app! It will be downloaded millions of times, and then I won't have to work anymore!"

Amy rolls her eyes and laughs. I have no coding experience at all, but as usual I am full of ideas.

"OK," I continue, "Money is not the meaning of life. What else ya got for me, guru?"

Amy drops another knowledge bomb on me, as if reading directly from some unseen self-help book. "Don't try to be better than others. Only try to be better than the person you were yesterday." I stop walking again and stare at her. "Wow. Who are you," I blurt out as I try to expand on this thought.

"I read that on Pinterest!" she laughs.

"I think I follow you, though," I reply with a smile. "So, let's see. We are out here walking to Santiago, but I have been feeling a sense of failure simply because we assume others are doing it better than us. Faster than us. Or more correctly than us." I pause in the shade of a giant beech tree. The base of the trunk is gnarled and as wide as a small car. "But what you're saying is, it is not about them or comparing ourselves to their journey. The meaning of life is simply improving yourself?"

"You got it," she replies.

"OK, so far we have love and don't try to be better than others. One and two. Any more meanings of life?"

We decide to take a break, sitting on a bench on the side of the road. The trail has followed a paved road thus far, and as we stop, our line of thought is interrupted by something that sounds like a large crowd. As we listen, a bit confused, a giant group of high school kids rounds the corner. They keep coming and stream past us like a line of human ants. There must be at least 100 kids walking by, our solitude interrupted by the buzz of chatty youth.

We let them pass and give them time to get far enough ahead, so we can't hear them. Finally, we strap on our packs and continue on. "So, where were we?" I ask. "Any more meanings of life?"

"I have a couple more that I have been thinking about. How about, cultivate peace?" she says. I mull over the thought in my head. "That one you are going to have to explain."

"No matter the circumstances of your life, find peace in yourself," she says. She sees me struggling to make sense of this and continues, "You know! Make your own weather. You were injured. We had to stop. You can choose your reaction to the circumstances. You can be angry, throw a pity party and stew in your miserable story. Or, you can choose to learn from it, grow and cultivate inner peace." I understand perfectly now, nodding my head in agreement.

I guess this is why so many cultures have a pilgrimage of some kind. You suffer a little bit physically and give yourself the time to learn the lessons you need to learn, breaking out of the routine of your life. "Why were you holding out on me?" I jokingly tell Amy. "You had the answers to the meaning of life all along!"

I am excited about these lessons and promise myself to focus on them when I get home. A task that I know will be hard to do. We arrive in Vega de Valcarce after a much easier day of walking than normal. I can't feel my heartbeat in my feet, and my typically swollen limbs are not swollen. My Achilles' tendon did not snap either, so I count today as a big success.

We check into a small albergue with only eight bunks in one room. We meet our amazing hospitalero named Matt. A true Brit, he offers us a cup of tea while we check in and get our passports stamped. He walked the Camino de Santiago a few years ago and then decided to quit his desk job in London, move to Spain, and open a pilgrims' hostel. He invites us to hang out after we have dinner in the common room upstairs, and we accept, promising to return in an hour or so.

At the restaurant next door, we dine on fresh garlic stuffed trout and a giant bowl of lentil stew. After the meal, we head back upstairs to find that a few more pilgrims have checked in including Melinda, a woman from Boulder, Colorado, in her late 50s. She is one of the people here who does not have a set schedule and doesn't know when she will finish. She is taking it slow and enthusiastically explains her journey so far.

"I carried 7 pounds of oatmeal with me from the states," she laughs. "You know you packed too much in your Camino pack when you have to pay for overweight luggage charges at the airport!"

"How was your meal?" Matt asks Amy and me.

"The trout was really good!" I reply. "He told us it was fresh. He stuffed the fish with garlic, which is never a bad idea. Do you ever eat there?"

He laughs and replies, "I am good friends with the owner. He wasn't lying when he told you it was fresh. He takes his fishing pole down to the river every morning and catches a few trout for the restaurant. If he doesn't sell them, he eats the fish himself."

We are all sipping more hot proper British tea with milk. "Why is that funny, though?" I ask.

"Because it is illegal! So don't tell anyone," he motions an imaginary key locking his lips sealed. "The Spanish government is worried about the dwindling numbers of fish in the streams here in Galicia. You're supposed to have a license, and there is a limit. Let's just say my friend is neither an environmentalist nor someone who really pays much attention to the law. Things run a little differently here in Spain. Something I am slowly getting used to."

After a great night getting to know Matt and Melinda, we head downstairs for bed. Amy writes in the Camino journal: *It was kind of hard to jump ahead of everyone and be surrounded by new and unfamiliar faces but I'm so happy we are taking a more relaxed approach to the last 10 days.*

Tomorrow, we climb a giant Galician mountain, which will be a challenge I hope my body can take. One thing is for sure, I know the views will be spectacular. Lying on the bottom bunk after lights out, I mull over the meanings of life we discussed today. I try to mold them into something almost tangible, tiny thoughts I can hold in my hand and stow away for later. In our barely populated room, sleep comes quickly tonight. Much needed rest comes as we get ready for another day on the trail.

Soul of Galicia

It is a cool, crisp morning, and as the sun rises, slowly revealing the landscape, I can tell we are in for a gorgeous hike. Lush green mountains and valleys filled with puffy damp morning clouds surround us. The clean, cool air fills my lungs with energizing oxygen.

"My body feels pretty good today," I say while examining my heel. The swelling has almost completely gone away.

"Knock on wood," Amy replies. I can tell she is happy with the news. "Let's see how you feel when we get up there," she says pointing to the top of a giant green mountain.

We begin a fairly steep climb on a heavily wooded trail and begin to snake our way through a dense forest. This is the first true test for my rested legs. I begin to put weight on my left knee to see if it will hold. So far, so good. My body struggles to trust my brain as it fights my attempts to walk normally.

As we continue to climb, completely alone, I hear a loud bark form somewhere up ahead. The animal seems to be getting closer and closer. All of a sudden, a giant German Shepard with a spiked collar and no owner emerges from the woods. The dog slowly approaches us on the trail. He looks angry, bearing his gnarled teeth, and immediately, my nerves are completely on edge. He is growling, barking, and will literally not let us pass him on the trail. I try to think of a solution. I have some nuts in my pack, which might appease the dog and make him like us.

I whisper to Amy, "What should we do? Should I hit him with Dolores?"

Amy quickly whispers back, "No, you idiot! That will make him angrier! Don't make eye contact, and we will walk forward slowly."

We move ahead at a snail's pace, tensely, as the dog continues with us for what seems like miles. My heart rate has accelerated as I mentally wish the dog away. He continues to walk ahead of us turning to observe these two scared humans every few minutes.

I wonder if he is the reincarnation of one of the Christian knights who would sometimes escort pilgrims through the most dangerous parts of these woods. Charged with guarding them from the Moors whom they were battling for religious control of Spain.[1] The dog has now seemed to adopt us and walks ahead, scanning the thick dark woods for would be attackers. My nerves calm a little. He no longer growls at us but only at the ghosts hidden behind fallen logs, bushes, and tree trunks.

Finally, as if called by an imaginary owner, the dog leaves us alone, and a wave of relief washes over us both. We continue through the forest until we are above the trees and clouds. It is now just us, a giant blue sky, and amazing views of the green mountains of Galicia all around.

We make it to a small village, O'Cebreiro, at the top of the mountain and stop for some lunch. This village is dotted with Celtic looking buildings made of dark gray stones topped with roofs of tightly woven straw. The famous dish of this region is *pulpo*, octopus, normally served with some smoked Spanish paprika, salt, and drenched in olive oil. We order a large wooden plate full of *pulpo* and wash it down with two *claras con limon*, or drinks made by mixing beer and lemon soda. The octopus is good but not my favorite as it takes on the feeling of chewing on a rubber tire after a while. I feel slightly nauseous after such a strange meal.

It is here in O'Cebriero where Don Elias Valiña Sampedro, the local parish priest who died in 1989, came up with the idea to mark the Camino de Santiago with the now iconic yellow arrows. They are the modern day guide that marks the many routes to Santiago.[2]

This is a popular stop for pilgrims after such a steep climb, and upon seeing the line outside of the albergue, we decide to continue on. We slowly walk through the rare Galician sunshine away from town, enjoying the views and the peculiar signature buildings of this region. The landscape is dotted with cattle and goats. Scots pine mix with oak and birch trees as far as the eye can see, only interrupted by squares of farmland cut out of the forest.

By three o'clock in the afternoon, we make it to the tiny village of Hospital de la Condesa and check into the Albergue Xunta. A Xunta is a government-run albergue, and this one has about 20 bunk beds in a large cold room. The building is in the middle of several pastures and connected farms. I do my laundry in the sink outside accompanied by a curious chicken.

It is colder here in Galicia, and since we threw Amy's sleeping bag in the trash in León to get rid of the bed bugs, I offer Amy my sleeping bag for the night. I simply lie on the bottom bunk wrapped in my rain jacket, still wearing my hiking clothes. When I wake up, I am a little confused. It felt like a nap, and I am already dressed. We unceremoniously head out the front door and start walking.

"I can see my breath!" I yell ahead to Amy. Unsurprisingly, she doesn't reply. I can barely hear myself as the raindrops constantly fall on the hood of my rain jacket, drowning out all other noise.

It is about 7 a.m., and the day has begun with heavy rain and thick fog. The light from our headlamps is filled with thousands of tiny raindrops speeding towards the ground. Even with our rain gear, we are soaked before breakfast. This combined with a steep climb over a trail covered with slick muddy rocks makes for a challenging early morning. We stop at the first bar we see and are greeted by a roaring fire and a kind smile from an elderly lady who treats us as if we are family. I look around the cozy room and on the wall see her picture in dozens of newspaper articles about the Camino de Santiago. We must have stumbled upon a gem.

I hang my wet rain jacket next to the fire and head up to the bar. We order thick toast with butter and spread rich dark brown local honey over the bread. The honey still has bits of pollen in it and has a strong smokey flavor. The kind woman offers a smile and tells me in Spanish, "The flavor comes from the bees who love the chestnut trees in this forest."

White steam is rising from our rain jackets as the crackling fire warms our bones. The hot coffee warms our souls. It is hard to head back out into the rain, so we spend more time than usual savoring our breakfast. "Would be a good day to stay inside and watch movies," Amy says, thinking out loud.

"That sounds amazing!" I reply, sitting next to the fire.

Reluctantly, we continue on. The rain slowly lets up, and after a few hours, we pass through a small Galician farm town. Out of nowhere, a woman appears from inside of a stone farmhouse, carrying a piping hot plate filled with fresh crepes. We take two, and she shakes some sugar on top. I ask how much and she tells us donation only. We fork over a few euro, she asks us where we are from, and after a few minutes we continue on our way. "Buen Camino, peregrinos!" she yells after us.

"Muchísimas gracias, Señora!" I yell back and wave.

I smile at Amy. I have never been so happy walking in the rain. We continue on through lush green forests and clouds until the sun finally starts to peek through and the thick fog starts to clear. We can finally see our surroundings. The Galician weather is almost teasing us, revealing the landscapes as if for only us to see, then covering them up again with another puff of cloud.

Today is turning out to be a good food day. We have been enjoying each region's style of food as we have made our way through northern Spain over the past few weeks, and today Galicia is making an argument for my favorite. Through the Basque region, in the beginning of our trek, it was *pintxos*. Here in Galicia, the warm hearty food seems to be designed for the weather.

We stop just before Triacastela and scarf down some delicious warm Galician stew, *caldo gallego*, made of white beans, greens, broth, and potatoes. We follow that with café con leche and *Tarta de Santiago*, the famous almond cake of Santiago. These little cakes are all topped with a powdered sugar imprint of the cross of

St. James and the Galician recipe dates back to the Middle Ages. We scarf down the history forkful by forkful before heading out the door.

After another hour or so, we come upon a thick raspberry patch with a table and small containers full of raspberries next to it. A box with a sign that reads, *Frambuesas 1 Euro* is sitting on the table next to the containers. A trusting store with no one to make sure you pay! Keeping karma on our side, I pop the money in the box and enjoy the juicy berries as we continue on.

After passing quickly through Triacastela, we soon find ourselves in another thick forest. The trees form a green tunnel over the trail, which blocks out the sun and spotty rain. We have not seen any pilgrims for an hour or so, and by about 3 p.m., we stumble upon an albergue. A simple sign painted in white letters in the dark red wood above the door reads, *Albergue el Beso*. There is no village here, only this modest gray stone building surrounded by a small patch of farmland carved out of a thick ancient forest. The roof is covered with dark wet slate, which looks like the slick scales of a giant black dragon. An amazing oasis in the middle of the forest. We check in, are led downstairs into a basement that is dark, musty, and damp, and have our choice of bunks as we are the only people here so far.

The relaxing energy is palpable and after a quick shower, nap, and some laundry, we both head outside. I find a giant swing hanging from an 800-year-old tree on a hill above the albergue. Plants grow from branches and emerald green ferns sprout up from every possible surface in the dark rich soil. I am beginning to understand why they call this leg of the Camino the spiritual section. I sit in silence, rocking slowly as the swing sways in the wind. Listening to the forest, I am filled with a reassuring sense of calm, and all stress melts away.

"Are you guys hungry?" a friendly voice pierces the solitude startling me. We are invited into the upstairs portion of the building, which is the owner's home, for dinner. "Come in, come in," a woman says, greeting us at the door. "My name is Isabel," she says.

She is holding a rosy-cheeked baby who stares at us with dark brown eyes.

"Nice to meet you! I am Gabriel, and this is Amy," I say as we take off our shoes and enter the home. There is a large wooden table set for dinner, and their home looks like the scene of some Hollywood romantic comedy. The walls are made of large dark brown stones, the floors unpolished wood and as we enter I glance into the kitchen. There is a wall with large shelves built in. Each shelf is full of Ball jars filled with all kinds of pickled vegetables. There is a large counter in the kitchen that is overflowing with fresh veggies, dirt still clinging to them as they were just plucked from the garden. There is a giant block of Manchego cheese on another counter and garlic hanging from the wall.

"I'm Jacob," a tall blond man, the cook, extends his hand. "I'm the husband. Please, welcome, dinner is almost ready," he smiles while motioning us into the main room. He looks like he is Scandinavian and his accent is definitely not Spanish. He has almost perfect English.

In the large open living room, the dinner table is set next to a large window that opens to an amazing view of our lush green natural surroundings. It has started to rain, which adds to the feeling of comfort as the sound of raindrops hitting glass fills the room. Someone has just lit three tall white candles that add a warm glow to the table and walls. Multi colored plates and dark green bottles filled with wine are lined up neatly on the table. Wonderful aromas from the kitchen swirl around the room making my mouth water.

It is one of those nights where the stars align and the conversation, company, and food are all incredible. We are joined by a German woman and another woman from Slovenia named Tezka. Two pilgrims who have just arrived and have decided to stay here for the night. The final dinner guest is a man from England named Art who lives just down the road. We all sit at the table and dig in. The owners, Isabel and Jacob, share an amazing story about meeting on the last day of their Camino de Santiago journey years earlier.

"We met in Finisterre on the beach. That place where many pilgrims go, you know, to burn their clothes and jump into the ocean," Jacob explains.

"We had our clothes on! We were both staring into the ocean and started to talk," Isabel finishes his sentence. "I thought he was very handsome but he told me he is from Denmark which made me sad."

"Where are you from?" Amy asks.

"Spain. From here in Galicia actually," Isabel replies.

"But it didn't matter. Our connection was so strong we decided to stay in Finisterre for a few more days before going home. We talked about the Camino and our adventure. What we had learned. How we had changed. And then," Jacob explains as Isabel jumps in again.

"And then the rest is history! We decided to open an albergue together. We wanted to continue to be a part of the Camino de Santiago every day. We chose this place because it is a perfect combination of solitude, living off the land and meeting people from all over the world every day," she says proudly.

Now they have a growing family. I glance at their new baby who scans the room with curiosity. A Camino baby.

"Did you name him Santiago?" I joke.

"No haha," Isabel smiles.

"Tezka," Jacob says turning to the woman from Slovenia and butchering her name. "Why are you walking the Camino de Santiago?"

"Well. I, um. I am trying to heal," She says. The mood at the table quickly changes as everyone senses a more serious note. "My brother died and my parents have also just died. My entire family is gone. They all died last year, and I have decided to walk the Camino de Santiago," she explains.

I recognize the same cloak of pain that surrounds her as I saw on Tom a few days ago. She seems to be farther along in the healing process, though, as a sort of joy emanates from her.

"I am trying to learn to live in the moment, and I want to let go. I have been so angry at life. You know. Why did this have to happen to me. I feel like it is unfair," She explains. It is completely dark outside now. The candles light the room as our shadows dance on the stone walls behind us. My face warm with wine, I share with her one of my favorite quotes about death. It is a little bit corny but I go for it anyway.

"What a caterpillar calls the end of the world, we call a butter-fly." —Eckhart Tolle, *The Power of Now*

"Has your walk helped?" Amy asks.

"Absolutely. I don't know how but I lost my anger somewhere along the Way. I am now making room for peace and acceptance of what is. What I can't change," she says. "I have actually been walking at night."

"What!?" There is a collective gasp at the table.

"Why at night? That must be really difficult and a little danger-ous," Jacob says.

"I don't know. Something has just been driving me to walk at night. I have been waking up at two in the morning most days and just walking in the dark. I haven't gotten lost yet. Or robbed," she smiles.

"Has it helped? Walking at night?" Amy asks.

"I actually fell yesterday. I dislocated my shoulder and had to pop it back into place," she says in a matter of fact tone. "If you could have heard my scream you would have thought I was giving birth or something. It was really painful."

"If that would have happened to me I probably would have died," I joke. She pulls up her sleeve and shows us the cuts and bruises on her arm.

"It has been sort of cathartic for me," she explains. "All of this physical pain has been good for my soul. I have pushed my body to the limit. But as this is happening my emotional pain is leaving me and has slowly been replaced by peace. I don't know how it is work-ing but it is healing me slowly."

"I can't imagine losing my entire family in the same year," Is-abel says.

"It is a lot. I have been through all of the stages of grief," she makes air quotes with her hands. "Mostly I have just been really pissed off you know. I have not been very pleasant to be around. And you, Gabriel, why are you here walking?"

I explain my search for purpose to everyone, and Tezka offers up some advice with the others.

"You know it sounds to me like you have been trying to become something or do things that others think is good. I used to do that too. My ego led me to a bank. I was a banker!" She laughs out loud. "Now I am a spiritual healer. Some people think I am crazy. I am a hippie now! But I finally decided to do what I want. Not what my friends think is great. Not what I think will make me somehow better than others. But what I want. You have a strong ego, Gabriel, I can tell. You have a kind soul so listen to that. Stop caring what others think. Stop trying to be better than everyone else."

"But what if I don't know what I want?" I reply.

"You do. You just haven't listened to it. You don't have the courage yet," she replies. "I will tell you what I tell my clients who come to me for advice. You may have already seen this advice in magazines or online. All day tomorrow while you are walking. Focus on one simple question. What would you do if you knew you couldn't fail?"

"That is good advice," Amy replies. Everyone at the table nods in agreement.

"How bout you, Art? How did you decide to live here in Spain?" Amy asks.

"I also walked the Camino de Santiago a few years ago and was inspired to quit my job in England and buy an old building out here in the woods. I love to paint so I decided to go for it. I turned my little building into an art studio, which is just down the trail," he explains in his thick British accent. "You should stop by in the morning."

A toast! Jacob raises his wine glass. "To what amazing things a long trek can do and may you all find your own way!"

I am buzzing with positive energy after our evening. Tezka is one of those people you meet that somehow make you feel better after spending time with them. I feel so good spiritually that I can barely sleep. Amy's entry in the Camino journal sums it up perfectly: *Today was one of my favorite days! Amazing place to stay with incredible energy and people.*

Tomorrow we continue through the forest. I can't wait to see what lies ahead.

Crowds

With well over 200,000 people walking the Camino de Santiago every year, it is inevitable that your daily hikes through nature can become a lesson in patience.[1] We have been lucky thus far and have been able to avoid the masses when we want. It has seemed like simply a popular trail in a typical national park. At some points, I have even questioned the statistics as I stare at a landscape void of humans. Only myself and Amy. I know this is all about to change.

The feeling of seclusion has been enhanced today by a persistent and thick fog. The trail is amazingly beautiful. We are alone on a dirt path and the branches of this old forest are so thick that they wrap over our heads, acting as a sort of natural umbrella protecting us from the rain. The only sound is the wind and the occasional drop of water that escapes the leaves and falls onto my rain jacket. The oak, chestnut, and beech trees have seen many pilgrims before us and will see many more generations long after I am gone.

My mind starts to think about our dinner conversation from last night. Why is it so hard to live in the moment? I tend always to focus on my next project or goal. This drives me crazy, but it is so hard to stop. If I only made more money. If I could only have more time to do things like this. If only I didn't get injured a few days ago. If only ... . During a break, I glance at our map to get our bearings and see a quote I needed to hear: *"The foolish man seeks happiness in the distance; the wise man grows it under his feet."* — J.R. Oppenheimer.

The trees seem to sway with approval as I read the words. I think about my injury a few days ago and the lessons I am trying to put into practice. It is not about comparing yourself to others. It is not about the destination. It is most definitely not about what could have been if my body didn't break. When there are literally no people around for me to compare myself to, it seems an easier lesson to learn. A sudden joy bubbles up from my chest turning itself into a smile. I think I might be getting the hang of this.

We continue on, making our way up, up, and finally above the trees and the clouds. The views today are spectacular and make it well worth walking through the Galician rain. As the hours pass, each trail looks like the cover of a meditation self-help book. I expect a troll, hobbit, or fairy to jump out from behind a moss covered log at anytime.

I am enjoying the solitude as much as possible because we are about to pass through Sarria. This is where the trail will become crowded. Sarria is the starting place for pilgrims who are short on time but want to receive the *Compostela* (the official paper that says you have completed the Camino de Santiago) once they arrive in Santiago de Compostela. The minimum requirement to receive the *Compostela* is 100 kilometers by foot, or 200 kilometers by bike.[2] Busloads of tourists are dropped off in this city, which is the first that meets the 100 kilometer walking requirement. We have heard that the number of pilgrims will increase exponentially after Sarria, and the trail can sometimes turn into a walking traffic jam.

Trying to avoid the crowds, Amy and I strategize and plan on staying in the villages just past or before the main stops listed in most guidebooks. The albergues are packed in these big cities, so avoiding the masses can relieve the crowd shock many pilgrims experience at this point. Because we have already spent a large portion of our budget on several hotels, luxury is not an option. The budget has suffered enough.

"If we ever do this again," I tell Amy, "we should bring a light two person tent!"

"Only if you carry it!" she jokes.

A small number of pilgrims do bring tents with them and instead of fighting for a bed and cramming into the network of albergues all along the Way, they stop next to the trail to set up camp. They simply throw up their tent and enjoy the silence, free of charge. The path of the Camino de Santiago aligns with The Milky Way and lying on your back outside of your tent, one can enjoy the 300 billion stars that shine overhead in an incredible cosmic scene. There is minimal light pollution to dim your celestial show. Some choose to walk at night for this very reason. The trail lit by stars.

We pass quickly through the streets of Sarria and make our way to Barbadelo. I do notice a slight change in the number of people on the trail, but it is not significant. As we rest on a log, a family of four passes by. They clearly have started their journey today, and their packs are gigantic. The kids are around seven and eight years old, and I can only imagine the multitude of extra things mom and dad must have to carry. They wear the excitement of a fresh new adventure and enthusiastically yell to us, "Buen Camino!!" as they pass.

"They smell good," Amy observes after they are gone.

"I know!" I reply. "I noticed that too! They smell like fresh laundry and soap." I sniff at my shirt.

"I wonder what we smell like to them?" Amy laughs.

"Let's just say if we met that family on the street in our current state anywhere else but on this trail, they might lock their car doors." I am only half joking while staring at weeks worth of toothpaste stains on my one long sleeve shirt. I need to stop brushing my teeth in the dark.

We eventually check into another Xunta Albergue, the only one for miles, which is run by the government of Galicia. Despite our plan to avoid the crowds, as we approach Barbadelo, I see a line of pilgrims waiting to get a bed. This is the first albergue line we have experienced so far, but luckily we do end up getting a bed. These places are dirt cheap, this one only 5 euro per night and popular because of it. Several people are turned away after we check in. The albergue is completely full. We head upstairs, and my mood instantly sours.

All of the bunk beds are pushed together with little space in between. As we enter the room, we squeeze by people to find a bunk. This can't be up to fire code, that is for sure. We are stuffed in the room like clowns in a tiny car. There is a group of young guys listening to some loud talk radio show not giving a damn that there are 30 others packed into the room. We try to take showers, and they are ice cold. Guys and girls shower in the same room as well which makes it interesting for Amy.

By bedtime I put my earplugs in and lie on my side ready for sleep. I find a large bearded man snoring right in front of my face. His bunk might as well be considered the same bed as mine. I can almost smell what he had for dinner, his breath making waves in the room. He has done nothing wrong, but still I despise him. I want nothing more than to be anywhere but here lying next to him and the other 30 people in this small room.

My claustrophobia is ironic as I shared a room with my mom until I graduated from high school. We had a bunk bed. I slept on the top bunk and she slept on the bottom. You would think I would be used to not having my own space. After our short time living in a tent, my mom was able to find a small place for us to live. This was before tiny houses were a phenomenon worth websites and documentaries about living with less. Before it was in style. But we lived in a tiny house. It was a home, with a roof, a wood burning stove and a small space for a bunk bed. You would think I could get used to these albergues.

Our 25th day on the trail promises the largest crowds yet. But not before a peaceful morning trek. We get an early start, and the sun's rays are spectacular this morning as we walk during yet another sunrise. The golden orange light cuts through the trees highlighted by the mist to form dozens of individual sunbeams. The sound of our walking sticks is absorbed by the clouds. The feeling of seclusion and peace is incredibly calming. In this setting, I couldn't stress myself out if I tried.

All along the Camino de Santiago we have noticed creative entrepreneurs who set up little food stands in locations that have particularly large gaps between villages. This morning, we decide to stop at one for the first time. Outside of an old stone barn, in the middle of nowhere, we see a nice looking woman who has hot coffee, fruit, and snacks. It is *donativo,* or pay what you want.

"Buenos días!" the woman greets us with a warm smile. She is wearing a thick colorful wool sweater, rubber rain boots, jeans, and has sparkling blue eyes.

We grab two coffees and decide to rest and chat while drinking from tiny plastic cups. Maria is from Italy and moved to Galicia recently. Another Camino transplant. We tell her about our journey so far, my injuries, and the people we have met. She is one of those people you just click with and has a vibrant soul.

"We are from Colorado," I say sitting on a big moss covered rock next to the barn. A heard of sheep starts to pass us slowly.

"Colorado!" She exclaims! "My brother lives in Colorado! He works on a pumpkin farm in Loveland. Do you know it?" I smile in acknowledgment.

"My mom lives in Loveland! Small world," I reply.

The sheepherder strolls up to our location following her sheep. She says something to Maria in the local Galician language, which I can't follow. They exchange a laugh, and then shepherd and sheep continue up the trail.

"There is a school group coming," she turns back to us explaining with a frown. I hear them before I can see them. A small rumble of conversation grows.

As if on cue, a massive group of 90+ high school and middle school students rounds the corner and descends on this little food stand like a swarm of locusts on a field of corn. Many taking advantage of the *donativo* and donate nothing. They all want a stamp for their Camino passports, and I watch Maria scramble to stamp a constant stream of papers with her unique Camino stamp.

Despite my efforts to be in a zen-like open-minded state on this trip, I find myself incredibly annoyed. The teachers finally come up behind the large group and offer a buen Camino. I frown. This is not the first school group I have seen on the Way, and each time, I have been equally annoyed at the chaotic interruption to my peaceful days.

When you are walking for religious purposes, to get over the death of a loved one, to discover the meaning of life, or for whatever the reason, when this pack walks around the corner with techno music blaring from cell phone speakers, it tends to piss you off. I am enraged at the treatment of Maria and her stand.

My wife Amy is a school psychologist and loves kids, so I turn to her to see if I am just being an unreasonable jerk.

"I know this is not my trail, not even close, but why the hell would you choose the Camino de Santiago as your school field trip?" I ask annoyed. Amy shoots me a look to say be quiet.

"Oh they speak Spanish and I hope they can hear me!" I say, my volume increasing.

"It is a historical trail," Amy replies. "A UNESCO World Heritage Site. I know it is annoying but I am sure the teachers are just trying to bring a local history lesson to life."

The crowd finally passes completely, and Maria is clearly a bit rattled. I would be, too, if my pay what you want business model was just devoured by a mob. I ask her what she thinks of this.

"This is a new phenomenon on the Camino de Santiago," she replies. "You never used to see school groups, and many locals think it is another way of turning this sacred trail into a tourist attraction. Especially when there are so many other amazing hikes in Spain that would work for a field trip." I nod in agreement.

We say our goodbyes after letting the noisy group walk ahead for a while and pop some euro in her wooden *donativo* box. I am thankful for our chat with this stranger. Our slow pace has allowed us time to have these unrushed improvisations.

Hours pass back on the trail. Unfortunately, there are even more giant school groups crowding the Way, and they are singing. I am in a bad mood, listening to a group of school kid's versions of

Lady Gaga and trying my best to focus on learning patience or any kind of lesson from this. I just want them to go away and be quiet. We work to find gaps between the school groups and try to walk in these quiet pockets of solitude. I notice other pilgrims, haggard looking from weeks on the trail like me, who are doing the same.

"Stop being such a grumpy old man!" Amy snaps at me as I glare at yet another group we let pass.

"I can't help it!" I reply. I decide to stop wanting silence and at least embrace conversation with other pilgrims. Amy has a point, and I need to change my mood. She has a habit of doing this.

My mind wanders back two years in the blink of an eye. I have a hoodie on in our small apartment in the middle of Granada. It is January, and as usual, our apartment is freezing because electricity is too expensive in Spain, and I am too cheap to turn on the heating. It also happens to be our birthday. Our birthday because Amy and I happen to have the same birthday.

"What is the matter with you?" Amy asks.

"I am freaking depressed," I reply from under a blanket laying in the dark on the couch in the living room. "I am 30, Amy! 30! I also found a gray hair! I am dying in front of your eyes!"

"So what?" she replies. "When you are 40, you will wish you were 30. When you are 60, you will wish you were 40, and when you are 120 you will be dead and won't have the chance to worry. Here." She hands me a cupcake. It is from a particularly amazing bakery in town. "Happy birthday."

She always manages to do something special even though I piss and moan every year. I hate birthdays. For someone who hates to be reminded of his own mortality, birthdays are the worst. A sick way to remind you that you have one less year to live on this Earth.

"Happy birthday," I reply. Instantly I am filled with gratitude for her. My other half. I know that no matter what, she is the best thing that has ever happened to me. Something that actually matters and if all else goes to crap it will still be enough.

"Seriously, stop being such a drama queen," Amy snaps me out of my daydream as the school group has finally passed us on the trail.

We continue on and throughout the day meet a virtual traveling United Nations. We meet people from South Korea, Poland, Australia, England, Ireland, and more. Each person here for a unique reason. I continue to be pleasantly surprised by what an international experience this is. You truly are walking with the world. The human experience and the struggles people come here to work through and walk through have a very common thread. Money problems, loss, anxiety, relationship difficulties, religion, life crisis, all answers to the most common question on the Camino de Santiago, "Why are you here?"

When we finally make it to Portomarín, we sit down to rest at an outdoor café and order a pitcher of ice cold sangria. As we sit, Tezka from Slovenia, whom we met a few days ago at the albergue El Beso in the middle of the woods, pulls up a chair at our table. I love these random second meetings, and we enjoy a drink and refreshing conversation. I soak up her words as she seems to be a sort of spiritual guru who also has been sent here to teach me not to be such a grumpy old man.

There is a straggler from one of the school groups outside throwing an absolute tantrum as her teacher or dad begs her to keep walking. She refuses, and the battle rages on while everyone pretends not to stare. They argue in Spanish.

"Nooooooooooooooooooooo!!!!!" the girl screams at the top of her lungs.

"Por favor. Vamos!" the man pleads with her. *Please. Let's go!* His nerves are clearly frayed, and he looks exhausted.

"No camino mas!!" *I am not walking any more!!* She sits with her arms crossed on the bench outside. Tears are streaming down her face, which is red with teenage rage.

"Well. That is some birth control for ya," I glance back to Amy and Tezka.

"No kids?" Tezka asks.

"All of our friends have kids. Some have several already. But for us, not yet," Amy replies.

Our conversation turns to these school groups, and Tezka says she handles the annoyance by seeing herself in the school kids and remembering how she used to be. "They are simply on a different path and part of the Camino of life. If you see yourself in people it is harder to dislike them," she says.

"Gabe throws fits like that every year for his birthday," Amy jokes. We both laugh. She has a point. Living in the moment, Tezka decides not to stay here for the night so continues on after our drink. Who knows if we will ever see her again, and we exchange hugs before she walks off into the afternoon sun.

After being turned away from several full albergues, we eventually score a room in a small albergue with only four beds. Translation: a good chance of sleep tonight!

This small village, situated next to a giant reservoir, feels very Scottish. As we are dining on a delicious dinner of lomo with *pimientos de padron* (small green peppers fried in olive oil), we hear bagpipes playing in the town square. We head towards the music to find a small group playing bagpipes and drums as the sun begins to set on this incredible scene. Pilgrims dine outside of the multiple restaurants that surround this central plaza. The sound of the bagpipes echoes off the medieval looking Romanesque church of Saint Nicholas, which has managed to catch the last rays of today's sun. A little boy rides his bike zigging and zagging over the cobblestones, imagining the crowd is watching him.

"Happiness, not in another place but this place ... not for another hour, but this hour. Walt Whitman," Amy says out of nowhere.

I turn to look at her and ask, "Since when do you quote Walt Whitman? Are you on Pinterest?"

She points at the guidebook, "I cheated."

"Wise man," I laugh.

We sit simply enjoying the music. And taking Mr. Whitman's advice, I shut off my mind. Soon the sun is down, and the musical group parades out of the square, pilgrims slowly follow suit, making their way to bed, the music and crowds fading along with the day.

The Pencil

Trail Day 27

"Happy 4th of July!" Amy jokes. The fog is thick today, and we can't see very far ahead on the trail. I am starting to grow fond of the fog of Galicia. It is like a calming security blanket that eases you through the day.

"Happy 4th!" I reply. "Feels like we are a long ways away from the U.S. of A!"

The sun eventually starts to burn off the clouds and the day gives way to the heat of summer by the afternoon. My knee pain has returned, reminding me to take it easy and giving me something new to worry about. We may be close to our destination, but there is still a long way to go. Sleep deprivation, constant pain, drying clothes on my backpack, and not shaving for 27 days now is increasingly turning me into a sort of homeless looking hiker. My hat has been soaked too many times with rain and is sort of sagging off my head in a sad worn state. I feel a lot like my hat today.

We decide to stop for lunch at a busy trailside bar and are surprised when Aaron, one of our Australian friends whom we met at the beginning of our Camino, sits down next to us! I did not think we would see him again because of my injury break in Léon.

"How is it possible that you caught up to us!" I asked actually wanting to know. "Did you take a bus?"

"No, no. Training, mate. Training," he replies in his thick Australian accent.

We devour a bocadillo and fresh squeezed orange juice as he tells us about a hike he took in Papua New Guinea a year earlier called the Kokoda Trail. It's a sort of rite of passage for Australians, Aaron explains, "That hike tore me up. I was the last of my group to finish, and I was in so much pain that I cried several times."

In front of me, I see this tall, muscular man's man and have a hard time imagining him crying.

He continues, "I didn't train at all for the Kokoda Trail. So when I decided to walk the Camino de Santiago I spent every weekend walking with a heavy pack over long trails. Hours at a time. This time my body was prepared for the shock, and I am in good shape because of it."

I think about my training, which involved walking to *REI* from my house in downtown Denver to break in my shoes. That took about one hour. No wonder my body is in such bad shape.

When I first met Aaron somewhere near Pamplona, he was walking with a friend from Australia who he traveled here with named Blake. We shared dinners with them both as well so I am a little confused. We finish our breakfast and before continuing on I ask, "Where is Blake?"

He stares at his coffee and frowns his reply, "Thirty days is a long time to walk with someone, mate."

I decide to leave that one alone, and we say goodbye. We walk through thick woods over natural paths of dark soil for hours. It feels like walking through yet another idyllic emerald green Galician postcard.

We finally make it to Boente and check into what at first looked like a complete dive of an albergue. A few flies scatter as Amy and I enter, and we see a Spanish man with a huge salt and pepper beard in the corner. He is busy working on a computer. He notices us after a few minutes, and my lack of enthusiasm quickly fades as a huge smile spreads across his face.

His name is Hector and he welcomes us to his establishment, asking if we need a bed. We check in and are shown our room, which is small, containing only four beds. After a hot shower and nap, we head downstairs for dinner. Hector and his mother make us feel incredibly welcome and he gets to work making us a fresh plate of baby squid, lightly fried with garlic and olive oil. The meal looks a bit terrifying but the flavor is incredible.

After an equally amazing dessert, he sits down and a fantastic conversation ensues. He tells us to wait a minute as he walks into the kitchen, brings out a large brown ceramic dish and declares it is time for a *Queimada*.

"*Queimada*," Hector explains, "is a traditional Galician drink to be shared among friends. You are my new friends, and I am happy you are here in Spain spending your evening with me."

The drink is a sort of hot punch made from *Orujo Gallego*, which is a clear spirit distilled from wine. As he talks with passion about the Camino de Santiago, which he has walked almost 10 times, he pours a full bottle of the strong liquor into the pot. He follows this with a generous amount sugar and begins to stir. His mother, who must be about 80 years old, looks on with a mischievous grin on her face.

Hector stirs in fresh squeezed lemon juice and handful of whole coffee beans. He then lights it all on fire! A deep blue unnatural looking flame licks at the air above. The heat is like a little campfire, and we all gather round like city folk in the woods trying to get a picture of a rare animal. He hands the large ceramic ladle to Amy followed by a large scroll filled with words and tells her to read.

"What is this?" Amy asks unraveling the scroll of paper.

"It is a spell!" Hector explains. "It is in our language, Gallego, but I will translate. The purpose of the spell is to ward off bad spirits that surround you. We will get rid of the bad and invite in the good!"

"Is this like a witches brew or something?" I ask.

"Sort of. It will help you make it to Santiago in good spirits," Hector replies. "Read, read!"

Amy begins, "Mouchos, curuxas, sapos e bruxas. Demos, tras-gos e diaños, espíritos das neboadas veigas. Corvos, píntegas e meigas: feitizos das menciñeiras." Her words sound strange as she struggles with pronunciation. The lights are dimmed, and Hector translates for us all. Firelight dances on the walls of the room.

"She said ... Owls, barn owls, toads, and witches. Demons, gob-lins, and devils, spirits of the misty vales. Crows, salamanders, and witches, charms of the folk healer." Hector is enjoying this im-mensely and so am I. "Now, use the spoon to lift some liquid and poor it back into the pot."

She follows his direction and as she pours a stream of blue fire slowly drips from the ladle back into the pot. A trick that any bar-tender would be proud of. Amy continues her spell for a few min-utes as we all stare into the fire.

"Pecadora lingua da mala muller casada cun home vello. Aver-no de Satán e Belcebú, lume dos cadáveres ardentes, corpos muti-lados dos indecentes, peidos do infernais cus, muxido da mar em-bravecida." She continues on. The translation making us all giggle like adolescent boys.

"Sinful tongue of the bad woman married to an old man. Satan and Beelzebub's Inferno, fire of the burning corpses, mutilated bodies of the indecent ones, farts of the asses of doom, bellow of the enraged sea." Hector's voice is deep and theatrical and he also smiles as he translates the word *farts*.

Hector stirs the cauldron as it continues to cook our strange brew. His mother clearly approves.

Amy makes it to the end of the spell before we can take a drink. "E cando este beberaxe baixe polas nosas gorxas, quedaremos li-bres dos males da nosa alma e de todo embruxamento. Forzas do ar, terra, mar e lume, a vós fago esta chamada: se é verdade que tendes máis poder que a humana xente, eiquí e agora, facede que os espíritos dos amigos que están fóra, participen con nós desta Queimada."

Hector passes out small ceramic mugs to us all as he translates the end, "And when this beverage goes down our throats, we will get free of the evil of our soul and of any charm. Forces of air, earth, sea, and fire, to you I make this call: if it's true that you have more power than people, here and now, make the spirits of the friends who are outside, take part with us in this Queimada."

Hector then fills all of our mugs, and we settle into a seated circle with our drinks. The warm sweet flavored brew is delicious. We all sit in thought for a while and are then joined by three more pilgrims who must have been napping upstairs. A mother, daughter, and aunt from Australia whom I have seen off and on over the past few days on the trail.

"El Camino de Santiago," Hector begins. He wants to tell us a local's perspective on the Camino and how it has changed. Amy translates his Spanish for the threesome of Australian girls. Hector continues with passion speaking with his hands for emphasis. I wonder to myself if he does this every single night with pilgrims.

"Unfortunately most establishments see you all as euro or dollar signs as you walk," he emphasizes the international sign for money by pointing his fingers to the sky and rubbing them together. "Most of the food you have eaten until now is not the best Spanish food. They make for you what is cheap and profitable and I should know because I have walked the Camino de Santiago many times!"

The thought is sad, but I guess I understand. As with anything that is growing with popularity, it is hard to keep the authenticity of an experience. To me, it makes finding the hidden gems all that more special.

This particular Spaniard has traveled the world and his philosophy is to treat travelers as he likes to be treated when he is in a foreign country. This includes fresh food, making you feel at home, and sharing a part of your culture. I love this guy. He shares stories about the Galician culture as he refills our delicious hot drink. We all cup the drinks with our hands as if huddled around a campfire.

"Escucha," he says. *Listen.* His tone turning serious. "Despite all of this. The Camino de Santiago is the greatest journey in the world. I am the man I am today because of the Camino." All of us in the room nod enthusiastically thinking about our own journeys thus far and what we have learned.

"The Camino de Santiago is like a pencil." He holds up a pencil for effect. "Each of us is like a dull pencil when we begin the journey. Just like this pencil. Sure, it writes! But not as well as it could."

My face is getting warm from the strong drink, but I am completely engrossed in his analogy.

"The Camino de Santiago sharpens you into your greatest and truest form. A better version of yourself. You are all better versions, more true versions of yourselves than when you started walking a few short weeks ago," he explains.

I hope he is right. I want him to be right, but I think it will take some time for me to truly understand how the Camino de Santiago has changed me. Wood shavings fall to the ground as he begins to sharpen the pencil. I look down at the shavings on the floor and a wave of understanding hits me. Why do I see pivots and failures as a bad thing in my life? My failures have made me into the person I am today. A person who finds himself in the middle of Spain learning from a grand adventure. A person who feels out of place on the path most traveled. I like that person. My physical challenges on the Camino were just a few chips, shavings, falling to the ground. Another event that softly whispers hey, remember why you are here. Remember and grow from it. I am the product of divorced parents, a black eye birthmark, baseball, travel and many career paths. All experiences put in my path to make me a little better. That is if I choose to learn from them. I too often choose to panic.

Hector grabs a piece of paper and slowly writes, "El Camino de Santiago."

"See!" Hector holds up the paper to show us all the words. "Now this pencil is a better version of itself. Sharp and focused. The best it can be."

He hands me the pencil before saying goodnight. It is almost 11:30 p.m.

"Gracias, Hector," I say. "This has been a really incredible night." He pats me on the shoulder and gives me a look as if to say, *good luck my friend,* before we all head off to bed.

Life Stages

It is 6 a.m., and I look at myself in the bathroom mirror. My half closed, sleepy eyes bolt open when I see my reflection. "Oh shit!" I blurt out.

Blood is smeared all over my face. I look at my hands, which are covered in blood too. "What the hell!" I mentally scan my body for injuries or pain, and quickly I realize what has happened. Of all the nights so far on the Camino de Santiago, last night was by far the worst night's sleep. The entire night a seemingly endless barrage of mosquitos landed on any exposed part of my body and sucked my tired blood to their bastardly hearts' content. The constant buzzing around my ears keeping me awake. I must have killed a few of the suckers that had become slow from bloated, blood-filled stomachs.

I inspect myself again in the mirror and start laughing like a crazed serial killer. This of course makes me laugh harder. I clean myself up and head back to our room. The two girls from Israel in our room look tired, too, and they confirm the buzzing kept them up all night. "Mosquitos?" I ask Amy who is just waking up on the top bunk.

"Yeeeep," she replies in a grumpy tone. As if on cue, another mosquito buzzes by my ear. "Let's get out of here before we need a blood transfusion."

I booked a five star hotel before we came to Spain, and it is waiting for us in Santiago de Compostela. I cannot wait. We both drag ourselves outside into the forest to begin the day's trek. We soon find the trail enveloped by thick groves of eucalyptus trees and adopt a very slow pace continuing on in silence for hours. This has very much become the routine. A routine which I know I will miss when it is all over in a few short days.

"Is your spiritual pencil sharpening?" I ask Amy.

"I guess so. I hope so," she laughs.

Everyone we meet today seems to be dragging, too, as we are nearing the end. By late afternoon we make it to Salceda, a small village on the side of the highway. After checking into an albergue and scoring a four-bed room again, we shower and head downstairs. I am surprised to see our other Australian friend Blake (but no Aaron) and Sam the artist from London whom we haven't seen since just before Léon.

"I saw Aaron yesterday! I can't believe you guys caught us on foot. You are making me feel slow," I say to Blake.

"What did he say?" Blake replies.

"Who? Aaron?" I ask. Blake nods. "Oh, he said 30 days is a long time to walk together. That's all," I reply, sensing a fresh wound.

"Is that all! We got into a bit of a tussle right after we saw you." He is clearly angry. "It is so stupid really. We fought over the bottom bunk at an albergue, and the next morning I woke up, and he was gone. I guess I will see him at the airport when we get on the same flight back home."

We make plans for dinner, and after a few hours of napping, we meet up at one of the only restaurants in town. We end up sitting with a man from Latvia whom I judge to be in his late 60s.

"I am Henrick, nice to meet you," he says while shaking hands with everyone.

I don't even know where Latvia is exactly, but as usual, the human spirit is the same. If he makes it to Santiago on his planned arrival day, he will have finished the entire journey from France in 23 days! This without bus or taxi assistance. The man is a beast.

As we devour some much-needed calories and drink ruby red Spanish wine, he opens up about why he has walked the Camino de Santiago. He is a scientist and is thinking about changing things up and trying something new. "I am tired of the comfortable rut I have carved out for myself," he explains to the table. All of us are listening with our full attention.

"I love my life and wife of course. I enjoy my job as a scientist. But ... I ... I don't know, I ... ." He can't seem to find the right words to express his feelings.

I know the feeling well and finish for him, "But you are tired of the same ol', same ol'. You want something more. Something that matters more to you. A change?"

"Exactly. But it's different for me than for you," he replies and continues on as we all devour fried potatoes covered with olive oil and bits of *Jamón.*

"What do you mean?" Blake asks.

"I am in a later stage of life and—" We all shoot him looks of *you're not that old, what are you talking about.*

"No, really," he continues, sincerely wanting us to hear his point of view. "I am closer to the end of my life than you are. I am a scientist, and I think about life in that way. I don't care if I am getting older, I just am. I don't fear death at all. I look at it in a factual way and, well, leaving a respected job you have held for more than 30 years is going to shock so many people in my life. Including my wife and children."

"Yeah, but wouldn't they all just want you to be happy?" Sam asks as Blake tops off our wine.

"But it is my identity. My job is who I am," he replies in a sad, almost longing, voice. "Is it worth spending the time I have left on this earth, my final chapter, going back to school and starting from scratch with no guarantees? I am supposed to be retiring and relaxing like all of my friends. It is a tough decision!"

Is he crazy to change careers just before he retires? We all roll the question around in our heads as we ponder his dilemma. I think again about the pencil analogy we heard last night. The Camino has a way of helping you become a better version of yourself. "I think you should go for it," I blurt out. The others at the table nod in agreement.

"You know, yesterday Sam and I met a man who is attempting to complete the Camino de Santiago by wheelchair," Blake says. "He is paralyzed from the neck down and his friend volunteered to push him all the way from St. Jean to Santiago. They have already made it this far. Talk about bravery."

"They had a cardboard sign on the back of the wheelchair asking for volunteers to push for a while," Sam explains. "So we jumped in and pushed for an hour or so. It was so hard and his friend, the one that is pushing him, looked really, really tired."

Amy looks like she is about to cry. "That is amazing," she says.

Sam continues, "The man in the wheelchair was in such a positive place in life. What struck me was just how happy he was. You rarely meet people who are so full of joy. He couldn't stop smiling, and his story was pretty amazing. He wasn't born that way. He was in an accident, when he was in high school and for some reason his body keeps getting worse. But he is determined to make the most out of his life. He is a world traveler and has been more places than I bet anyone at this table."

"It puts things in perspective doesn't it?" Blake says.

"It does," Henrick nods in agreement and then says, "That is really quite inspirational. They are just going for it. Who cares what life says is possible and what is not."

"We are about a day away from Santiago. Has the Camino helped you come to a decision?" Amy asks.

He pauses and then replies with a slight smile, "I think so, yes. I really do think so."

I recognize the excited sparkle in his eye and already know his decision. Henrik is going to make a change.

I find comfort in other people's stories. Listening to Henrik's dilemma, I feel less alone. Less crazy. In him I see courage, not confusion. I remember the moments I knew it was time for a change in my life and how terrifying this can be. My radio career, which began with elation and the words, *I can't believe they are going to pay me to do this,* ended six years later when I had the courage to realize it simply wasn't for me anymore.

It was a Saturday morning when I had just introduced a Gwen Stefani song to the city of Denver. I edited a few videos for the station while songs and commercials played. I sat in the studio, miserable and confused. The passion was gone. I had already committed career suicide with my previous radio boss when I begged for a second chance then turned the second chance down. A few weeks after that I turned down my own night show at a big station in Denver. I wanted to focus on videos and hosting this weekend show as a sort of test to see if I could stomach radio anymore.

The program director, who offered me my own night show, looked at me as if I had stripped down naked and done the *Macarena* in front of him. "I'm sorry, did you say no thank you? Do you realize what I am offering you? This is your chance. Your shot at a major market radio job. I have a line of kids who will slit your throat for this gig!" The passion had been gone for a long time. I finally had the courage to admit it to myself and terror gripped my chest. If I wasn't a radio man, who was I? We decided to move to Spain to find out.

Santiago de Compostela

"I feel pretty good today," Amy says as she turns to gauge my response.

It is about 10:30 a.m., and we have already been on the trail for a few hours. "Me, too. I think today is the day," I respond with a big grin.

We are going to walk all the way to our final destination, Santiago de Compostela. I have a mix of emotions. I am sad, glad, happy, and everything in between. Above all, Amy and I are trying to enjoy the moment and soak in every second of the walk today as we make our way to the end.

We cross through forests and fields and over hills. We take our time snapping photos and taking advantage of old wooden benches and spectacular views. After hours of walking, we round a bend in the trail and finally get our first glimpse of Santiago de Compostela. We stop in awe to stare at the miniature buildings below us connected by wide concrete roads.

"We made it!" Amy yells to the sky. The buildings looks like a collection of miniature dollhouses down below. Somehow they don't seem real.

It is a strange feeling to have been thinking about a destination for the past 30 days. Then when you actually see it, you want to feel elated. You want to have a moment where you cry and fall to your knees, the angels singing and people applauding your achievement. This, in fact, is what you have been looking forward to the whole time. But as we make our way into the city in search of the famous cathedral, where St. James himself resides in a silver tomb, I feel nothing but shock.

We have been in the serene, silent, natural beauty of Galicia for days and the bustle of the city is overwhelming. It is like spending a few hours inside of a dark room and walking outside into the bright light of midday. Your senses are overwhelmed, and it is hard to handle. People speed by, busy with the business of living their lives. Horns honk, and we blend into the sea of humanity.

We do eventually make our way to the city center, round the corner and just like that, find ourselves in front of The Cathedral of Santiago de Compostela. This massive structure was finished and blessed in the year 1211 and has seen thousands upon thousands of pilgrims over the years.[1] Today, it welcomes us.

There are weary pilgrims lying in the *Praza do Obradoiro* using their backpacks as pillows, staring up at the cathedral, much like me, in disbelief. Some are crying. Many are hugging each other. Still others look on with no emotion at all. Much like me, I wonder what exactly I am supposed to feel. There is a little tourist train slowly making its way into the center of the square. It looks like it is straight from Disneyland, chugging around us on small rubber tires over the old cobblestones. Tourists in the train are snapping pictures of the pilgrims like they are on safari, and we are the animals on display in our native setting.

I gaze up at the giant cathedral as the stone carving of St. James stares down from its perch up above, and I try to think of nothing at all. I focus on being completely here, in the moment, experiencing this with Amy. I feel relaxed and relieved to have made it this far. In total, we have traveled 788 kilometers, or 490 miles, in 29 days. We walked 655.8 kilometers, or 408 miles, and the rest we completed by taxi, train, and bus.

We see many of the people we have met along the Way in the square and say hello, but everyone seems to be lost in thought. No one seems elated as I would have expected. Maybe it is a sort of sadness that this is all over, and we have to go back to the real world. If nothing else, this has been a true adventure that I am truly grateful to have had.

"Well," I say, turning to Amy. We are both seated on the stone ground, staring up at the scene. "How ya feelin?"

"Good. I guess," Amy replies. She seems to be in the same state as I am. "Should I be crying? There are lots of people crying."

"I don't think you *should* be anything," I reply.

"Are we dead inside?" she jokes.

"I don't think so," I laugh. We both stare back up at the giant old cathedral.

The building is undergoing a restoration. There is scaffolding covering much of the front of the building with a giant picture of what you *should* be seeing. It seems somehow appropriate. I feel I *should* be wearing a sign myself that reads, "Restoration in progress thanks to the Camino de Santiago." I have not yet grasped the restoration, and it may take months to finally understand it all.

"Well, I know what I am feeling. I am feeling like I need to eat a big plate of *Jamón*," I tell Amy. "You hungry?"

"Now you're talkin," she replies.

We sit in the square for a while more, taking it all in before deciding to find a hotel and then dinner. What a day and what an adventure this has been. We have arrived a day earlier than we had planned so have to wait until tomorrow to check in to our five star hotel. It is 6 p.m. We decide we have had enough of albergues and choose a *pensión,* which is basically one step above a hostel and one below a hotel. The *pensión* is glorious. I have spent the last month drying myself with the little travel shammy towel I got from REI, and the giant white hotel towel seems like an extraordinary gift fit for a king.

The next day, we sleep in, enjoying the pillow top bed.

"Our last day in Spain," I tell Amy. My few words loaded with mixed emotions. It seems somehow unnatural waking up and not walking.

We will spend our last day attending the Pilgrim Mass, which takes place at noon inside the giant cathedral. I plan on using today to try and reflect on what has happened over the past 30 days. I also plan on eating every food that I love here in Spain before we leave tomorrow. That means *Churros con Chocolate* for breakfast. One thing I am not worried about right now is calories!

After a delicious breakfast, we make our way to the *Praza de Obradoiro,* the golden square of Santiago, to observe the new pilgrim arrivals and do some thinking. As we sit and take in the scene, I spot a familiar face in the crowd. The Barista and the Hungarian crew whom we met the first few days on the trail! We rush over to them to say hello, and I am so happy to see them.

"Still wearing my knee brace I see," The Barista jokes.

I smile and reply, "Did you find your answers on the trail?"

"I did. I will open the best coffee shop in the world when I get home," he replies with a look of excitement in his eyes.

After this, we see John from New Orleans and the woman from Boulder, Colorado, who carried 7 pounds of oatmeal with her along the Way! It is like a little Camino reunion right in the square. The Hungarians are planning to walk to Finisterre, the end of the earth, and I wish we had time to join them.

We then see Cole, the young priest in training we met on the hardest day of my journey. He enters the square with a big grin on his face.

"Hey! How are you guys?" he asks, surprised to see us. "You made it! Man, when I saw you, you had just learned you had tendinitis right? I didn't think you guys stood a chance!"

"You were pretty ill, too, right? From the bad soup the sisters fed you? Did the charcoal pills we gave you work?" Amy asks.

"You know that is a really funny story actually. Oh! Hold on a sec," he reaches into his pack and pulls out a folded piece of paper. "We wrote a poem about the charcoal pills. Can I read it to you?"

Amy and I look at each other with amusement. "Of course! Let's hear your poem."

"OK, here goes. Don't laugh. I am a budding poet and, well, your gift of charcoal pills inspired me. You wouldn't believe how much we talked about this," he clears his throat. The cathedral towers above him as more pilgrims pile into the square. His big grin leaves his face and he begins in a serious tone:

"The feast of the birth, the forerunner of Christ.
With the sisters full of mirth, we were being led by the Geist.
At Carrion de los Condes, we feasted on the soup.
The stomach then asked, donde estas?
Groans, rumblings and grumblings filled the group.
In Terradillos the first pilgrim dropped.
Oh sisters' soup, oh sisters' soup,
of what were you made, with what were you topped?
Oh sisters' soup, oh sisters' soup.
In Camino wrong turns are none,
what is a pilgrim without pain?
So we arrived with another stomach undone.
Oh sisters' soup, could we have refrained?
Calzadilla de los Hermanillos. Did we find a cure?
Yes, a pilgrims' pain is known by Dios, so he took the pills,
black and pure.
Oh sisters' soup, oh charcoal pills.
Across las Mesetas brown, burnt, sun and shade,
flats and hills.
One pilgrim to another, trust is learnt.
What is a pilgrim without pain? Songs and laughs.
Oh little black pills. At Villa Franca they raised cain.
Vomited up. Victory. Only despair kills.
So onward we go pilgrims.
Oh sisters' soup, oh charcoal pills.
We remember, we forget, singing hymns.
Oh sisters' soup, oh charcoal pills.
So important are our pains? No Lord, let us not think so.

With you we pilgrim even in the rains.
Oh sisters' soup. Oh charcoal pills.
To Santiago we go."

"Bravo!" Amy says as we clap enthusiastically. We are both grinning from ear to ear.

"Well done!" I say.

"Thanks, guys," Cole says with a shy grin. His face has turned red.

Seeing so many people that we met these past 30 days now here in Santiago brings me a sense of closure. All of them contributed, in some small way, to the lessons I will be taking home with me.

We say our final goodbyes and head to the Pilgrim Office to get our *Compostela*. The official certificate of completion for the Camino de Santiago. The criterion of a bona fide pilgrim is that you have walked at least 100 kilometers. We clearly qualify for ours and get there early before the lines start to form.

We check the boxes on a quick survey that asks questions like *Where did you begin? Where are you from? What are your reasons for walking the Camino?*

"Passports?" The friendly person behind the counter interrupts my scribbling on the form.

I show her my pilgrim passport, now full of colorful stamps collected along the Way, and they hand me my *Compostela*. It is a small official-looking scroll stating that I have completed the journey. After we leave, Amy notices that they spelled her name wrong. "Do you want to go back and get a new one?" I ask.

"No, it's fine," she replies. "It's only a piece of paper!"

I know what she means. The piece of paper seems empty and receiving it an anticlimactic experience. It feels as if we just went to the DMV and got a new driver's license.

We make our way to the cathedral at about 11:30 a.m. and take our time as we enter. The cathedral is immaculate, and the first thing you see at the front door is the *Tree of Jesse*. This ornate carved stone column is the work of the Master Mateo. Thousands of years of tradition has had pilgrims touch the stone column and send up a prayer of thanks for safe arrival. You can see where fingers have worn holes into the stone over the centuries. This work of art has been here since 1188.[2]

It boggles the mind thinking about how many pilgrims have touched this very stone over time. I wonder what a typical pilgrim in the 1200s was thinking about while standing here in this very spot. Unfortunately, you are no longer permitted to touch it for historical preservation purposes. Small makeshift metal barriers keep us away from the column.

Once inside, we make our way to the tomb of St. James. We get in line and slowly make our way down some steps into the heart of the cathedral under the massive altar. I turn to the left and see a small silver casket that contains the remains of St. James himself. You are supposed to kneel before the casket and pray or say a few words. I simply think, *Thank you, thank you for the lessons I have learned,* and just like that, my moment with St. James is over, and we walk away.

"That silver casket thing was really small," I whisper to Amy. "Were people tiny back in the day?"

"Maybe it was because he didn't have his head?" Amy replies. "Who knows."

We take our seats in an absolutely packed cathedral, which seats 1,000 souls. In front of us, we see the giant incense-burning *botafumeiro*, secretly hoping they will be swinging it through the air. This large silver vessel, about the size of a large vase, is held in the air by a giant rope that hangs from the very top of the church. The botafumeiro was originally used to fumigate the dirty, smelly, and sometimes disease infested pilgrims as they arrived.[3]

Unfortunately for us, the priests do not swing the vessel as often as they used to, and sure enough they don't swing it during our mass. It is a moving ceremony, though, as a tiny nun begins to sing, filling the cathedral with her angelic voice. Many pilgrims are crying, resting their heads on a neighbor as they weep. Most of us are simply lost in our own thoughts, listening to the sound of her voice.

The priest gives a moving message about the journey we have all just completed and many prayers of thanks are read in a multitude of languages for the international crowd. Eventually the ceremony comes to a close, and we all pour out into the streets of Santiago. After the mass, we decide it is time to check into our much-anticipated five star hotel.

After we soak our feet in the giant pool and steam our sore muscles in the luxurious sauna, I try to sum up the experience in my mind. What did I learn on this trip? Besides the meanings of life we discovered, I think back to the rock my walking stick Dolores fell on during day four which simply stated, "It's about the Way, not about the destination." The parallels with life are unmistakable.

"How ya doin over there?" I ask Amy. We now sit in our insanely luxurious room talking and enjoying a bottle of nice Rioja wine in celebration. We have both been lost in thought for a while, letting the lessons from the past 30 days wash over us.

"You know in yoga, they teach that all of us have something called dharma," she says.

"Of course you are thinking about yoga," I joke. "What does dharma have to do with our walk?"

"Dharma is basically your duty in life. Your calling. What you are supposed to be doing," she says.

"Your purpose," I chime in.

"Yeah, I guess so. I will have to learn more about it when we get home. Anyway, from what I have learned, in yoga your entire life is a pilgrimage meant to help you understand and find your dharma," she explains.

"You have to figure it out over a lifetime? It is not something you are born knowing?" I ask.

"For some it is easier of course. But yeah. The purpose of your life is to find your purpose," she says.

"The purpose of my life is to find my purpose. That is deep," I smile and hold up my wine. "To the Camino de Santiago."

"To a new way of life and to enjoying moments like this no matter what tomorrow might bring," my wise guru wife replies as our plastic hotel cups tap together.

I spent a lot of time over the past 30 days worrying about how and if we would make it to Santiago. In the end, we did in our own way. I started this journey wanting answers to my questions. I wanted to find my purpose. But I have learned something far more valuable along the Way. Maybe the purpose is the pilgrimage. I vow to return home and enjoy the Way, enjoy the imperfect journey of life no matter the goals I am trying to achieve or changes I am trying to make. I think of all of the people we met along the Way. All searching, growing, struggling. There is no future for them, no past for me. Only the frustrating, humbling, wondrous, and beautiful now.

It is time to start walking. I finally feel like I know how.

Day 22: Galician Mountains

Day 27: Mystical Sunrise

Day 28: Wooded Trail Galicia

Day 29: The Cathedral of Santiago de Compostela

Afterword

As with all life lessons, it is easy to forget. My *Live in the Moment* and *Enjoy the Journey* mantras quickly left me while waiting in line at the airport in Santiago. My blood was boiling because of some unseen delay, and I quickly realized how hard it would be to take my newly learned lessons home with me.

Upon return to the United Sates, physically I did not improve as quickly as I had hoped. Hip stiffness I experienced on the flight home turned into intense, lasting pain. I pushed my body to its limits and have sustained some long-term injuries that remind me every day of the Camino de Santiago and the respect it commands. My Achilles' heel is still stiff and feels weak at times. My knee, which caused me the greatest amount of pain, ironically has improved more quickly. For the rest of my body, it has taken five months of rest and slow rehabilitation to heal and to process this experience fully. Thankfully, almost six months later, my muscles, tendons, and joints are nearly back to normal.

Mentally and spiritually, the Camino de Santiago has left a lasting change, and after my initial airport tantrum, I now sense a monumental shift in my being. Even if I have not fully processed what this means. As is the case when you return from overseas, well-meaning friends and family ask the standard question, "So how was your trip?" I honestly respond with, "Life changing," and a select few ask for more details.

I did not plan on writing a book about this journey until some months after returning to the United States. The effort has been a great way to share the lessons learned and inspire others to do the same. It has also been a way for me to reflect and process these lessons, which are easy to forget once you come back to the real world.

The most important lesson is to live in the moment, and I've set the lock screen on my iPhone to remind me of this every day. A picture of the rock I stumbled upon in Spain that read *"It's about the Way, not about the destination."* When I look at it, I remember that life is happening now, so you best enjoy the ride.

A few days after the journey ended and I returned to the United States, it was back to work and the daily grind of a predictable 8 to 5 life. It was a shock to go from the daily adventure of trekking to making copies in an office in the same week. My mind drifts back to Spain and the call of adventure almost daily. I was looking for direction, purpose, and the answer to my career crisis on the Camino de Santiago, and I did not find an exact solution. Instead, I am focusing on the life lessons I gleaned from our time in Spain to cultivate peace, from which I hope I will find my answers.

Instead of pursuing jobs working for others, I am now focused on creating my own. For me, a huge shift in thinking. For purpose, I am finding meaning in the little things. During days where I feel insignificant, I remember how important small conversations were for me and how most of the people I met on the Camino have no idea how they helped me on my path. I remember that a simple charcoal pill can lead to a poem and that small acts of kindness really do matter.

Interestingly, Amy, who was not having a career crisis, has experienced a change as well. From a deeper understanding of self, she has decided to pursue a passion for yoga and enrolled in yoga teacher training a few short weeks after our return. This has turned into a possible new career shift. The Camino helped her see that the intense demands and emotional drain of being a school psychologist were leading to mental burn out, and she is giving herself permission to pursue other interests.

Let me offer a warning to anyone thinking about taking on the Camino de Santiago themselves. This experience will change you. Whether you are looking to heal from a divorce, getting over the loss of a loved one, looking for a grand adventure, or experiencing a semi life crisis like me, the Camino de Santiago has answers if you are open to hearing its messages. They may not be what you are expecting but, they are there now, waiting for you, and the souls you will meet along the Way will be your guides.

Buen Camino

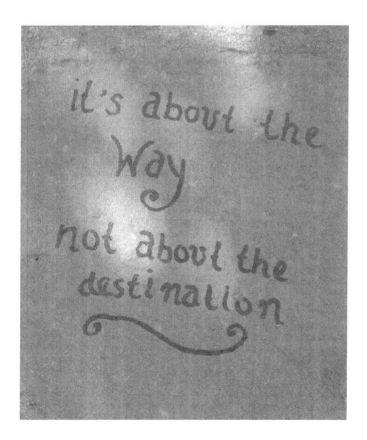

Endnotes

Introduction

1. Acts 12:1-2 (New International Version (NIV)).

2. John Brierley, *A Pilgrim's Guide to the Camino de Santiago: St. Jean – Roncesvalles – Santiago* (Forres: Camino Guides, 2014), 31-32.

3. Rufino Lanchetas, *Gramática y vocabulario de las obras de Gonzalo de Berceo, Volume 1* (Est. tipográfico: Sucesores de Rivadeneyra, 1900), 685.

4. Brierley, *A Pilgrim's Guide to the Camino de Santiago*, 32.

The Barista

1. Brierley, *A Pilgrim's Guide to the Camino de Santiago*, 67.

2. Instituto Nacional de Estadística, "Navarra: Población por municipios y sexo," http://www.ine.es.

Walking Stick

1. Pilgrim's Welcome Office, "Statistics," http://www.peregrinossantiago.es.

La Rioja

1. Pilgrim's Welcome Office, "Statistics."

2. Brierley, *A Pilgrim's Guide to the Camino de Santiago*, 107.

Camino Surprises

1. Asociaciones de Amigos del Camino de Santiago: Federacion Española, "In Memorian," http://www.caminosantiago.org.

Bed Bugs

1. Brierley, *A Pilgrim's Guide to the Camino de Santiago*, 123.

2. WebMD, "Bedbugs," http://www.webmd.com.

3. Texas A&M AgriLife Extension, "Insects in the City," http://www.citybugs.tamu.edu.

4. Brierley, *A Pilgrim's Guide to the Camino de Santiago*, 133.

5. UNESCO, "Burgos Cathedral," http://www.whc.unesco.org.

The Meseta
1. Brierley, *A Pilgrim's Guide to the Camino de Santiago*, 136.
2. Trading Economics, "Spain Unemployment Rate," http://www.tradingeconomics.com.
3. Pilgrim's Welcome Office, "Statistics."

Roman Way
1. Brierley, *A Pilgrim's Guide to the Camino de Santiago*, 148.
2. Lionel Casson, *Travel in the Ancient World* (Baltimore: Johns Hopkins University Press, 1994), 189.
3. Perseus Digital Library, "Smith's Dictionary of Greek and Roman Antiquities (1890)," http://perseus.uchicago.edu.
4. Brierley, *A Pilgrim's Guide to the Camino de Santiago*, 151.

Achilles Tendinitis
1. Brierley, *A Pilgrim's Guide to the Camino de Santiago*, 163.
2. Mayo Clinic, "Diseases and Conditions: Achilles Tendinitis," http://www.mayoclinic.org.
3. WebMD, "Fitness & Exercise: Achilles Tendon Injury," http://www.webmd.com.

Rest
1. European Economic Snapshot, "Spain: Still in the Throes of the Great Recession," http://www.europeansnapshot.com.

Soul of Galicia
1. Notre Dame Magazine, "History of the Camino de Santiago," http://www.magazine.nd.edu.
2. Brierley, *A Pilgrim's Guide to the Camino de Santiago*, 234.

Crowds
1. Pilgrim's Welcome Office, "Statistics."
2. Pilgrim's Welcome Office, "The Compostela," http://www.peregrinossantiago.es.

Santiago de Compostela

1. Lozano, Milan, *Camino de Santiago Inolvidable* (León: Everest, 1999), 235.

2. Brierley, *A Pilgrim's Guide to the Camino de Santiago*, 274.

3. Brierley, *A Pilgrim's Guide to the Camino de Santiago*, 274.

Bibliography

Acts 12:1-2. *The Holy Bible*. New International Version (NIV). Colorado Springs: Biblica, 2014.

Asociaciones de Amigos del Camino de Santiago: Federacion Española. "In Memorian." Accessed April 10, 2015. http://www.caminosantiago.org/cpperegrino/scriptorium/in memoriam.asp.

Brierley, John. *A Pilgrim's Guide to the Camino de Santiago: St. Jean – Roncesvalles – Santiago*. 10th ed. Forres: Camino Guides, 2014.

Casson, Lionel. *Travel in the Ancient World*. Baltimore: Johns Hopkins University Press, 1994.

European Economic Snapshot. "Spain: Still in the Throes of the Great Recession." Accessed April 14, 2015. http://euro peansnapshot.com/spain/.

Instituto Nacional de Estadística. "Navarra: Población por munici-pios y sexo." Accessed April 11, 2015. http://www.ine.es/jaxi T3/Datos.htm?t=2884&L=0.

Lozano, Milán. *Camino de Santiago Inolvidable*. León: Everest, 1999.

Mayo Clinic. "Diseases and Conditions: Achilles Tendinitis." Ac-cessed October 23, 2015. http://www.mayoclinic.org/dis eases-conditions/achilles-tendinitis/basics/definition/con-20024518.

Notre Dame Magazine. "History of the Camino de Santiago." Accessed April 14, 2015. http://magazine.nd.edu/news/1297-history-of-the-camino-de-santiago/.

Perseus Digital Library. "Smith's Dictionary of Greek and Roman Antiquities (1890)." Accessed November 1, 2014. http://perseus.uchicago.edu/Reference/antiquities.html.

Pilgrim's Welcome Office. "Statistics." Accessed November 15, 2014. http://www.peregrinossantiago.es/eng/pilgrimsoffice/statistics/.

Pilgrim's Welcome Office. "The Compostela." Accessed April 12, 2015. http://peregrinossantiago.es/eng/pilgrimage/the-compostela/.

Texas A&M AgriLife Extension. "Insects in the City: Bed Bugs." Accessed April 20, 2015. http://citybugs.tamu.edu/factsheets/biting-stinging/bed-bugs/.

Trading Economics. "Spain Unemployment Rate." Accessed April 6, 2015. http://www.tradingeconomics.com/spain/unemployment-rate.

UNESCO. "Burgos Cathedral." Accessed November 15, 2014. http://whc.unesco.org/en/list/316.

WebMD. "Bedbugs." Accessed May 20, 2015. http://www.webmd.com/skin-problems-and-treatments/guide/bedbugs-infestation.

WebMD. "Fitness & Exercise: Achilles Tendon Injury." Accessed April 10, 2015. http://www.webmd.com/a-to-z-guides/achilles-tendon-problems-topic-overview

Acknowledgments

This book would not be possible without a group of people to whom I must express my deepest gratitude. I am most grateful to all of my friends in Spain who first told me about the Camino de Santiago and helped me turn it from an idea into a reality. I am also thankful for all of the fellow pilgrims from all over the world whom I met along the Way. I am grateful for their openness and the personal stories they shared. Without them and the lessons I gleaned from their life experiences, the Camino de Santiago would not have been such an incredible journey.

I am profoundly grateful to Jonathan Ekstrom, a friend and fellow writer, who spent hours reading through this body of work, offering his time and helping me refine and find my voice. He was the first to read the manuscript, and when we met for happy hour to discuss the book, I was nervous to say the least. His honesty, feedback, candor, and willingness to challenge me to dig deeper helped transform this book.

To Bridget Verrette, a friend and editor, thank you for the generosity of your time. Your notes, suggestions, and talent made me feel like a better writer. To Dave Dickerson, an outdoorsman and friend, your perspective, encouragement, and notes were invaluable. To my copy editor, Agnes Bannigan, thank you for your enthusiasm, professionalism, kindness, encouragement, and for working with a brand new author.

Above all, I owe my thanks to Amy, my wife, for her constant support in the adventures of life. Your encouragement, raw honesty, and wise soul continually remind me to enjoy the journey of life. There are no words I could write that are sufficient so I will simply say, thank you, Amy.

I would also like to thank you, kind reader, for spending time with this book.

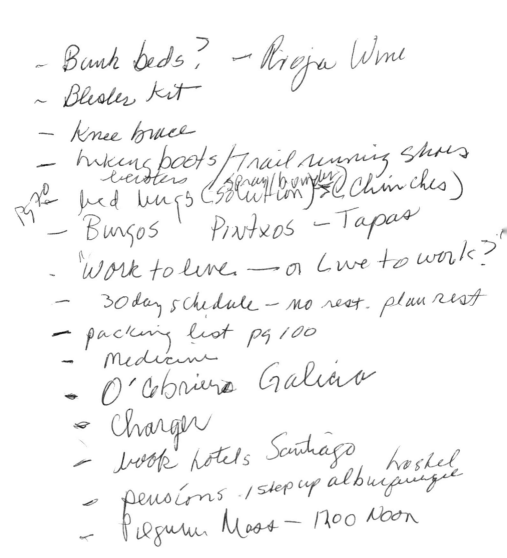

- Bunk beds? — Rioja Wine
~ Blister kit
- Knee brace
- hiking boots / Trail running shoes
pg 72 bed bugs (solution) (Chinches)
- Burgos   Pintxos — Tapas
- "Work to live. — or Live to work?"
- 30 day schedule — no rest. plan rest
- packing list pg 100
- Medicine
- O'Cebriero Galicia
- Charger
- book hotels Santiago   hostel
- pensions / step up albuquerque
- Pilgrim Mass — 1200 Noon

58020303R00106

Made in the USA
Lexington, KY
30 November 2016